November Gold

An Anthology of Poems

by

Wilfrid Wilson Gibson

November Gold

An Anthology of Poems
by Wilfrid Wilson Gibson

Edited by Hilary Kristensen

Published by Wagtail Press, Hexham
Northumberland, NE47 0HS
www.wagtailpress.uk

First edition 2018

With grateful thanks to Judy Greenway and the Wilfrid Gibson Estate
for their permission to reproduce this collection of poems.

A special thank you to Dr Roger Hogg for sharing his vast knowledge of
Wilfrid Gibson and his work, and for his help and encouragement.

Homecoming - An earlier collection of Wilfrid Gibson poems
was published by Wagtail Press in 2003.

ISBN 9780955939549

Printed by Biddles - www.biddles.co.uk

CONTENTS

EVERYDAY FOLK

WORKING LIFE

MYSTERY AND IMAGINATION

NATURE & COUNTRYSIDE

THE TWO WORLD WARS

FRIENDS & POETS

AT SEA

INTRODUCTION

November Gold has been published to commemorate 140 years since Wilfrid Wilson Gibson's birth in 1878 – and to present an anthology to a new generation of readers as well as those familiar with Gibson's poems.

Known as an author of war poetry and such classics as *Flannan Isle* and *The Golden Room*, Gibson also wrote with great understanding and emotion in the voice of early twentieth century working men and women. His characters seem to come to life through his words – meet Bessie Stokoe, Betty Riddle and Ralph Lilburn, go to country fairs and markets – and trudge across moorland with a shepherd and his dog.

As Gibson loved his native Northumberland with its ruined castles, wilderness and Roman history they feature in many of his poems.

Making a selection from Gibson's work, which spans almost fifty years, has not been easy as there are so many to choose from; I hope this collection will appeal to those who already know his verse and to readers who would like to discover an enjoyable introduction to Wilfrid Gibson and his poetry.

Wilfrid Gibson's punctuation and original spelling have been retained in this anthology – whenever possible from first editions of his books; however, as all of his original publications are out of print, books of collected poems have also been used for reference.

Hilary Kristensen
Editor

FOREWORD

It is over fifteen years since the editor of the Wagtail Press brought out *Homecoming*, a selection of Wilfrid Gibson's poems; in my foreword to that volume I welcomed the enterprise as making Wilfrid Gibson's poems newly available.

November Gold, another selection from Gibsons's huge output, is to be equally applauded as making a poet, whose work is out of print, readily available to a new public.

Born in Hexham, at 1, Battle Hill Terrace, on 2nd October 1878, Gibson was a prominent poet in the early and mid-twentieth century. The house in which he was born was demolished long ago but a surviving carriage-entrance archway, with a window above, carries a memorial plaque reminding us that this was the Gibsons' house.

The family was a large one: the parents, seven children – five daughters and two sons –together with two living-in servants. There had been Gibsons in Hexham since the sixteenth century; one ancestor operated the West Boat Ferry on the Tyne. John Pattison Gibson, Wilfrid's father, was possibly the most prosperous and distinguished of his family. He owned the family business, a dispensing chemist, in Fore Street, which also dealt in photographic and optical materials. He had been a member of the local militia, was internationally renowned for his antiquarian and photographic work for which he was awarded many distinctions. His wife, Elizabeth Frances Judith Walton, was from Newcastle; she died in 1902 and John Gibson subsequently remarried, aged 69. In 1907 he brought his new wife into the family home – a local woman whom the children heartily disliked. At this point Wilfrid left home to live in a very poor area of Glasgow where he forged a new sense of his poetic mission.

Up to that time, very much influenced by his eldest sister, Elizabeth, and the taste of the period he had written a fanciful style of poetry, not much connected with the workaday world. Glasgow changed all that and he became the spokesman of the urban poor and took an interest in the new Independent Labour Party. Elizabeth was a published poet in her own right and had had considerable influence on her young brother whose private schooling appears to have been very patchy.

After fifteen Gibson had no further formal education, but with his father he travelled extensively at home and abroad, remembering stays in France, Palestine and Alexandria with its "harbour crowded with sails."

After his Glasgow sojourn Gibson returned for a while to Hexham but felt that "humanly speaking, the atmosphere was all wrong." As he had made literary contacts in London he packed his belongings and took the train south: He was then 34 years of age and had half a dozen books in print. It was the best move he could have made.

Once in London he was helped to get a small attic room in the Poetry Bookshop in Devonshire Street, run by the poet Harold Monro. There he met other writers including Rupert Brooke and Edward Thomas and the young French sculptor Henri Gaudier-Brzeska, all three of whom died in the Great War.

Monro's secretary at the Poetry Bookshop was a young woman from Dublin who had spent three years at Newnham College, Cambridge: Geraldine Townshend was a very good secretary and Monro was quite annoyed to lose her when she married Gibson. This took place at her family home in Dublin in 1913. "What an absolutely perfect husband he should make" wrote D.H. Lawrence, who had earlier said of Gibson "he is the dearest and most lovable person I know."

Through the influence of his friend Lascelles Abercrombie, Gibson and Geraldine left London for Gloucestershire to live in a cottage called The Old Nailshop, in the village of Dymock, which became a writers' colony. There, the Gibsons' first child, Audrey Greenway, was born in May 1916. In 1918 when Gibson was serving in the Army Service Corps – on home duty not active service – their son Michael was born. Then in 1920 a second daughter, Jocelyn Kielder, completed the family. Both Michael and Jocelyn survived into old age, but Audrey's life ended young and tragically. She had married in 1938, a German, Ali Hübsch, and they had a son, Roland; but in 1939, on the eve of the Second World War, Audrey was killed in an Alpine avalanche incident.

The Gibsons were naturally distraught, and when war was declared on 3rd September, Hübsch returned to Germany, being a German citizen and left the baby to be brought up by the grandparents.
At the end of the war the father laid claim to young Roland but the Gibsons were unwilling to give him up.

A legal battle was settled in the Court of Chancery and the grandparents were made guardians until Roland was 'of age'. He was educated at King's School, Canterbury and, when he left, went to join his father, then living in Canada.
Geraldine, the heroine of the Gibson family and its great tower of strength, succumbed to pneumonia in 1950. Their life together had had an idyllic start but her later life became very burdened. After her death Wilfrid Gibson, by no means a capable manager of his affairs, lived with his son and his wife in Surrey. His years spent living in the south of England had been largely dictated by their children's educational needs and proximity to publishers and editors who could provide him with reviewing and publication. He longed, though, to be back in the land of his heart's desire, Northumberland, and contemplated "running away" to live in lodgings in the Borders

Just to see the rain
Sweeping over Yeavering Bell
Once again!

Just to see again
Light breaking over Yeavering Bell
After rain!

Yeavering Bell 1918

By the time of his death in 1962 Wilfrid Gibson had out-lived his appeal and was unable to get published. "The Old North Country Rhymer" as he described himself, was out-dated in a changing literary world. He felt that nobody wanted to read his work. How delighted would the poet of *Battle*, published in 1915, been to think that 140 years after his birth, 56 years after his death and in the centennial year of The Armistice, that a selection of his work is now available from the Wagtail Press.

Dr Roger Hogg
Newcastle Upon Tyne

FAMILY AND HOME

THE LONELY ROAD

So long had I travelled the lonely road,
Though now and again a wayfaring friend
Walked shoulder to shoulder and lightened the load,
I often would think to myself as I strode –
No comrade will journey with you to the end.

And it seemed to me, as the days went past
And I gossiped with cronies or brooded alone
By wayfaring fires, that my fortune was cast
To sojourn by other men's hearths to the last
And never to come to my own hearthstone.

The lonely road no longer I roam :
We met, and were one in the heart's desire :
Together we came through the wintry gloam
To the little old house by the Greenway home
And crossed the threshold and kindled the fire.

Dedicated to Geraldine Gibson
The Old Nail-Shop, The Greenway, 1914

FOR G

All night under the moon
Plovers are flying
Over the dreaming meadows of silvery light,
Over the meadows of June
Flying and crying –
Wandering voices of love in the hush of the night.

All night under the moon
Love, though we're lying
Quietly under the thatch, in the silvery light
Over the meadows of June
Together we're flying –
Rapturous voices of love in the hush of the night.

THE STAIR

Dear, when you climbed the icy Matterhorn,
Or braved the crouching green-eyed jungle-night –
With heart exultant in the sheer white light
Of the snow peak, or cowering forlorn
In the old Indian darkness terror-torn –
Had I no inkling on that crystal height,
Or in the shuddering gloom, how on a flight
Of London stairs we'd meet one Winter's Morn ?

And when we met, dear, did you realise
That as I waited, watching you descend,
Glad in the sunlight of your eyes and hair,
And you the first time looked into my eyes,
Your wanderings were done, and on that stair
I too, O love, had reached the journey's end ?

WHIN

Sweet as the breath of the whin
Is the thought of my love –
Sweet as the breath of the whin
In the noonday sun –
Sweet as the breath of the whin
In the sun after rain.

Glad as the gold of the whin
Is the thought of my love –
Glad as the gold of the whin
Since wandering's done –
Glad as the gold of the whin
Is my heart, home again.

ONE-DAY-OLD

Baby asleep on my arm,
Would that my heart could enfold you,
Cherish you, shelter you, hold you,
Ever from harm.

Born in a season of strife,
When warring with fire and with thunder
Men wantonly shatter asunder
All that was life –

Into a world full of death
You come with a gift for the living
Of quiet grey eyes and a giving
Of innocent breath.

Baby asleep on my arm,
Would that my heart could enfold you,
Cherish you, shelter you, hold you,
Ever from harm.

1916

AUDREY

On the sea's edge she dances –
Her glistening body bare
Amid the light foam glances,
Foam-light with tossing hair,
Eager for all that chances
By land or sea or air.

She dances yet undreaming
Of life's oncoming tide :
Yet when wild waters streaming
Surge round her deep and wide
Her soul foam-light and gleaming
Shall every danger ride.

TO AUDREY

Audrey, these men and women I have known
I have brought together in a book for you,
So that my child some day when she is grown
May know the frienxdly folk her father knew.

Wondering how parents can be so absurd,
Perhaps you'll take it idly from the shelves
And, reading, hear, as once I overheard,
These men and woman talking to themselves.

And so find out how they faced life and earned,
As you must earn one day, a livelihood,
And how in spite of everything they learned
To take their luck through life and find it good.

And maybe as you share each hope and fear
And all the secrets that they never told,
For their sake you'll forgive your father, dear,
Almost for being so absurd and old.

And may it somewhat help to make amends
To think that in their sorrow and their mirth
Such men and women were your father's friends
In old incredible days before your birth.

MICHAEL

Why should he wake up chuckling ? Only hark !
Chuckle and chuckle, lying in the dark
Alone in his little cot. What may there be
That we for all our wisdom cannot see,
Gazing grave-eyed, in the old heart of night
To fill his baby heart with such delight ?

TO MICHAEL

Dear Crystal-Heart, I pray that you
May do what I set out to do,
Easily and happily attain
What I have striven for in vain,
All that, for some infirmity
Of soul, life has denied to me.

May you breathe out as some blithe bird
All that my heart awaking heard
And laboured daylong to express
Through cloudy passion and sharp stress
Till gushing from its crystal spring
Your song in all men's hearts shall sing :

And in that music clear and true
Even I at last attain through you.

JOCELYN

As one who finds in dews of dawn
The crystal of the sprinkled lawn
Printed with hoofmarks of a faun,
That under the new moon all night
Has danced in circles of delight –
So I with thrilling heart surprise
The elfin light that gleams and glances
In Jocelyn's enchanted eyes
As her wild spirit dances, dances . . .

A GARLAND FOR JOCELYN

I
Little flame that barely kindled
Flickered low,
Little flame that paled and dwindled
As we watched you, grieving so,
That the life our love had wakened
To the dark again should go.

How we strove and strove to win you
From the night,
Till the baby-spirit in you
Slowly conquered, burning bright,
And the jealous shades were scattered,
And our hearts were filled with light !

II
When I think of you I see
A flame-winged fritillary
Glancing over daffodils.

When I think of you I hear
Leaping laughing amber-clear
Sun-enchanted rills.

III
Lively as a trout,
Flashing in and out
The golden mesh of sunlight
That nets the silver river –

Darting here and there
Through the dewy air
My little lassie frolics
With laughing life aquiver.

IV
When you dance
Amber-bright the sunbeams glance
In your tossing hair ;

So your name
Calls to mind a little flame
Dancing in the air –

Little flame for ever dancing
In the rain-washed air of April,
Amber flame through crystal glancing.

V

A charm of goldfinches
That flutter and flicker
Over daffodils flashing
Through sunshiny showers –

The light of your laughter
Flashes out of the silence
Though you have been sleeping
In dreamland for hours.

THE WIND-BELLS

Listening to the glassy tinkle
Of the painted Japanese
Wind-bells swaying in the breeze,
Michael sees
Butterflies of light that twinkle
Round the walls with golden glancing,
Glancing, dancing to the ringing
Of the crystal wind-bells swinging.

As he stands there listening, dreaming,
Fairer even than the flight
Of the butterflies of light
Flit the bright
Fancies in his blue eyes gleaming –
In his happy heart a rarer,
Rarer fairer music singing
Than the wind-bells' crystal ringing.

BY CARMARTHEN BAY

Behold the happy three,
Wading knee-deep through windy hyacinths
Against a beryl sea !

Dearest, if only we
Might hold them ever thus in idleness
Of April innocency !

Ah no ! not so, not so !
Rather, 'tis our exceeding happiness
To watch our children grow –

Springing and burgeoning
In the sweet light of heaven, or storm-beset,
Still bravely flourishing ;

Gaining from winter's stress
No less than from the idle summertide's
Full golden blessedness ;

And as, in love with life,
They swiftly grow to man – or womanhood,
Even more ours, dear wife –

Even more surely ours
Shall be their wise young hearts, than when they played,
Flower-like, among the flowers :

While still, in memory,
Three happy children among hyacinths
Shall frolic by the sea.

NORTHUMBERLAND

INSCRIPTION ON
HEXHAM'S MARKET CROSS AND FOUNTAIN

O you who drink my cooling waters clear
Forget not the far hills from whence they flow,
Where over fell and moorland year by year
Spring, summer, autumn, winter come and go,
With showering sun and rain and storm and snow
Where over the green bents forever blow,
The four free winds of heaven ; where time falls
In solitary places calm and slow.
Where pipes the curlew and the plover calls,
Beneath the open sky my waters spring
Beneath the clear sky welling fair and sweet,
A draught of coolness for your thirst to bring,
A sound of coolness in the busy street.

Hexham, February 1901

NORTHUMBERLAND

Heatherland and bent-land –
Black land and white,
God bring me to Northumberland,
The land of my delight.

Land of singing waters,
And winds from off the sea,
God bring me to Northumberland,
The land where I would be.

Heatherland and bent-land,
And valleys rich with corn,
God bring me to Northumberland,
The land where I was born.

DUNSTANBOROUGH

Over the unseen September tide the mist
Sweeps ever inland, winding in a shroud
Stark walls and toppling towers that in the cloud
Of streaming vapour soar and twirl and twist,
Unbuilded and rebuilded in grey smoke
Until the drifting shadowy bastions seem
The old phantasmal castle wherein man's dream
Seeks shelter from time's still-pursuing stroke.

And I recall how once above a sea
That under cold winds shivered steely clear,
Fresh from the chisel, clean-cut and white and hard,
These towers, rock-founded for eternity,
Glittered when Lancelot and Guinevere
One April morning came to Joyous Gard.

DEVILSWATER

Up the hill and over the hill,
Down the valley by Dipton Mill,
Down the valley to Devilswater
Rode the parson's seventh daughter.

Her heart was light, her eyes were wild –
Seventh child of a seventh child –
Down the valley to Devilswater
Came the parson's black-eyed daughter.

Down she rode by the bridle-track,
Down she rode, and never came back –
Never back to the Devilswater
Came the parson's black-eyed daughter.

Up the hill and over the hill,
Down the valley by Dipton Mill,
High and low the parson sought her,
Sought his seventh black-eyed daughter.

He tripped as he trod the bride-track,
A bramble tore his coat of black,
And he stood on the brink of Devilswater
And cursed, and called her the devil's daughter.

Up the hill and over the hill,
Rode a black-eyed gipsy Jill,
Down the valley to Devilswater
Rode the devil's black-eyed daughter.

Rode in a yellow caravan,
By the side of a merry black-eyed man ;
Down the bank to Devilswater
Rode the devil's merry daughter.

Her heart was light, her eyes were wild,
As kneeling down with her little child,
She christened her bairn in the Devilswater –
The black-eyed brat of the devil's daughter.

Low she laughed – as she hugged it tight,
And it clapped its hands at the golden light
That glanced and danced on the Devilswater –
To think she was once a parson's daughter.

FALLOWFIELD FELL

Soldier, what do you see
Lying so cold and still ?
Fallowfield Fell at dawn
And heather upon the hill.

Soldier, what do you see
Lying so still and cold ?
Fallowfield Fell at noon,
And the whin like burning gold.

Soldier, what do you see
Lying so cold and still ?
Fallowfield Fell at night
And the stars above the hill.

CLATTERING FORD

What did you hear at Clattering Ford,
Last night, as you lay by the Black Line Burn ?
Only the swish of a brandished sword,
And a heavy thud in the fern.

What did you hear as you lay in the ling,
Last night as you lay in the ling alone ?
Only a splashing of hoofs, and the ring
Of flying hoofs upon stone.

What did you see as you lay last night,
Last night as you lay in the ling and the fern ?
Only the moonlight silvering white
The waters of Black Line Burn.

THIRLWALL

In the last gleam of winter sun
A hundred starlings scream and screel
Among the ragged firs that stand
About the ruined Peel.

Bright singing birds of gold they were
To me when last, a little boy,
I came from Thirlwall, and they shook
The very sky with joy.

Still in that gleam of winter sun
A hundred starlings scream and screel
For ever in the ragged firs
About the ruined Peel.

WITCH'S LINN

We lay all night in Witch's Linn
Beside the Lewis Burn,
And heard the whispering of the wind
Among the withered fern.

We lay all night in Witch's Linn
Beneath the staring stars,
And the yellow horn of the old moon hung
Beyond the naked scars.

We lay all night in Witch's Linn
Till morn broke bleak and grey –
O that my heart had ceased to beat
Before the blink of day !

For evermore in Witch's Linn
I hear the Lewis Burn,
And the whispering, whispering, whispering wind
Among the withered fern.

SKIRLNAKED

O came you by Skirlnaked
When you came o'er the moor ?
And did you see an old man
Standing at the door ?
And did you see an old man
Glowering at the door ?

O came you by Skirlnaked
When you came o'er the moor ?
And did you hear a young bride weep
Behind the fast-shut door ?
And did you hear a young bride greet
Behind the fast-shut door ?

MOTHER AND MAID

And where be you stravaging to at such an hour of the night ?
To look on Allen Water in the full moonlight.
Go your wilful ways then ; but you will learn too soon
That no good comes to any lass from looking on the moon.

And where be you stravaging to at this unearthly hour ?
To hearken to the hoolet that hoots by Staward Tower.
Round the Peel at midnight the brags and horneys prowl,
And no good comes to any lass from listening to the owl.

So don't say I've not warned you whatever may betide.
And what should I be fearing with Robert at my side ?
What should you be fearing ? Since the world began
No good has comes to any lass from walking with a man.

NORTHERN SPRING

O skein of wild-geese, flying
Through April's starry blue,
Your harsh and eager crying
Searches through and through
My heart till it takes flight
Arrow-like with you
To pierce the Northern night,
Shedding flakes of light
From wings of flashing white
Through tingling airs a-quiver
On tossing waves that shiver
Crystal berg and floe –
On crashing ghylls and forces of winter's
                                      melting snow.

When down the water-courses
The spate of April dins,
Like hoofs of countless horses
Thunder the threshing linns
As leaping 'twixt the scars
Bright froth spurts and spins

And sprays the leafing spars
Of woods that rake the stars ;
And shattering bonds and bars
My spirit pours in thunder
Of torrents, trampling under
Dead winter's slothful dreams,
Till life's a singing tumult of April-
                wakened streams.

ON CAWFIELDS CRAG

So old the curlew seems,
Grey, lean and ancient, with his curving bill,
So rich and mellow his clear April call
From hill to hill,

That, listening to that voice
Whose very beauty moves my heart to tears –
The beauty only ripening wisdom brings
With the full years –

It almost seems to me
Believable the Roman sentry heard,
Standing on Cawfields Crag as I stand now,
That very bird.

THE WIND AND THE RAIN

Roman, Roman, what do you here ?
Your great Wall is fallen this many a year –
Fallen, fallen, the Roman Wall ;
And green grow the bent and the moss over all

The wind and the rain have tumbled down
What the foeman left of tower and town.
Well and truly you builded your Wall,
But the wind and the rain are the masters of all :
Bravely you builded :   but all in vain
Man builds against the wind and the rain :

The raking wind and the seeping rain,
Whatever man builds, unbuild again.
Man builds in vain, for the wind and the wet,
The water that saps and the airs that fret,
His pride of towers will overset.

Man builds : but all must fall as the Wall
You builded, O Roman, to breast the squall :
The wide-flung ramparts and cities tall,
Must fall as the Wall – yea, all must fall,
And the tempest ride over the ruins of all :
For the wind and the rain are the masters of all.

JOHN PATTISON GIBSON

Dead as the Romans he adored,
My father lies –
Yet can I see the light to his keen eyes
Leap, as the glitter of an unsheathed sword,
When, to the clarion of their names, awoke
His proud and eager spirit ; and he spoke
Of Hadrian's Wall, that strides from hill to hill
Along the wave-crest of the Great Whin Sill.

And surely now his spirit stands,
This crystal day,
When the first curlew calls, and bent and brae
Awaken to the spring, above the lands
Of his heart's love, on Winshiels' windy height,
With eyes that see the rampart, squared and white,
New-builded, as when Hadrian first surveyed
Rome's arrogance against the North arrayed !

THE ARROWHEAD

I stirred a mole-hill with an idle foot,
And caught a sudden glint ;
And, stooping down, among fine soil I found
An arrowhead of flint –

An arrowhead shaped by the cunning hand
Of some poor lad, long dead,
Some lad who'd lived, and loved, and fought – and left
Only an arrowhead –

Only a little flake of sharpened flint
That he had knapped with care –
The sole memorial of his hopes and fears,
His courage and despair.

And I – what shall be left of all my toil
When I yield my last breath ?
Nothing but words that for a little while
May linger after death.

THE CROWBERRIES

The crowberries on Cheviot
Were rare and hard to find ;
And bitter were they on the tongue ;
And yet, love, to my mind,

Because we sought for them together
In the still gold October weather,
No fruit of the Hesperides
Could vie with those harsh crowberries.

IN HEXHAM ABBEY

Like spirits resurrected from the tomb
We stept from the dark slype's low vaulted gloom
Into the transept's soaring radiancy
Where from the lancets of clerestory
Noon-sunshine streaming charged the pale sandstone
Of wall and pillar with a golden tone
Rich as the colour of the rock, fresh-hewn
From sheer Northumbrian hillsides to the tune
Of clinking hammer and chisel, in the days
When the aspiring spirit in life's praise
Soared in exultant fabrics of delight –
Earth quarried stuff exalted to the height
Of man's imagination, heaven-entranced.

And, as with eager footsteps we advanced
Through the South Transept with enraptured eyes,
From off our hearts fell the perplexities
Of these calamitous times ; and we forgot
Awhile the warring of nations and the lot
Of the battalioned youngsters doomed to march
Into annihilation – pier and arch
Springing in sunshine seeming still inspired
With the adoring ecstasy that fired
Those early craftsmen :   and we recalled how man,
Builder and breaker since the world began
Betrayed by frailties of the mortal flesh,
Is yet a phoenix soul that springs afresh
Resilient to the imperishable gleam
Out of the self-wrought havoc of his dream,
From devastation fashioning anew
His vision ; and that to his best self true
Man, the destroyer, is Man the builder, too.

THE STELL

The stones with which I build the stell
Were quarried by a Roman hand,
Longer ago than I can tell.

From sea to sea, across the land
The Romans built their great Wall well ;
And so I've stones right to my hand
To build a shelter for my sheep.

The Romans built the Wall to keep
The Northern tribes in their own land :
And so I've stones right to my hand
To build a shelter for the sheep
When winter winds blow keen and snell,
And blizzard sweeps across the fell.

The Romans built their great Wall well
Along the Whin Sill's craggy steep :
But they are gone ; and only sheep
And shepherds and their kinsfolk dwell
In the wild land they thought to keep.

The Romans came, and fought, and fell :
And so I've stones right to my hand
To build a shelter for my sheep.

EVERYDAY FOLK

THE ORPHANS

At five o'clock one April morn
I met them making tracks,
Young Benjamin and Abel Horn,
With bundles on their backs.

Young Benjamin is seventy-five,
Young Abel, seventy-seven –
The oldest innocents alive
Beneath that April heaven.

I asked them why they trudged about
With crabby looks and sour –
"And does your mother know you're out
At this unearthly hour ?"

They stopped :   and scowling up at me
Each shook a grizzled head,
And swore ; and then spat bitterly
As with one voice they said :

"Homeless, about the country-side
We never thought to roam,
But Mother, she has gone and died,
And broken up the home."

RALPH LILBURN

The night we took the bees out to the heather,
The sealed hives stacked behind us, as together
We rode in the jingly jolting cart, were humming
Like the far-murmuring rumour of blown branches.

White in the moon-flame was the flowering heather
And white the sandy trackway, as together
We travelled, and a dewy scent of honey
Hung in the warm, white, windless air of midnight.

A silvery trackway through moon-silvered heather
To the humming dark of the hives we'll ride together
For evermore through murmurous dewy midnight,
My heart, a hive of honey-scented moonlight.

THE OLD PIPER

With ears undulled of age, all night he heard
The April singing of the Otterburn
His wife slept quietly and never stirred,
Though he was restless and must toss and turn ;
But she kept going all the day, while he
Was just a useless bundle in a chair
And couldn't do a hand's turn – seventy-three,
And crippled with rheumatics . . .
                                        It was rare,
Hearing the curlew piping in the dark !
'Twas queer he'd got his hearing still so keen.
He'd be sore bothered if he couldn't hark
To curlew piping, shrill and clear and clean –
Ay, clean, that note !
                              His piping days were done,
His fingers numb and stiff : and by the peat
All winter, or all summer in the sun
Beside the threshold, he must keep his seat
Day-long, and listen to the Otterburn
That sang each day and night a different tune.
It knew more airs than ever he could learn
Upon the small-pipes : January to June,
And June to January, every hour
It changed its music. Now 'twas shrilling clear :
In a high tinkling treble with a power
Of mellow undertones : and to his ear
Even the spates of winter over stones

Made no dull tuneless thundering ; he heard
No single roar, but half-a-hundred tones
Eddying and swirling ; blending, yet unblurred ;
No dull-edged note, but each one razor-keen –
Though supple as the sword-blades interlaced
Over the morris-dancers' heads – and clean !...
But, nay, there was no word for it. 'twas waste.
Of breath to try and put the thing in words,
Though on his pipes he'd get the sense of it,
The feel – ay, even of the calls of birds
He'd get some notion, though low-toned a bit –
His humming drone had not that quality
Of clean-cut piping : any shepherd lad
Upon his penny-whistle easily
Could mimic the mere notes : and yet he had
A gift of feeling, somehow . . . He must try
To-morrow if he couldn't tune his pipes,
Must get his wife to strap them carefully . . .
Hark, a new note among the birds – a snipe's –
A small-pipe's note ! . . .

     Drowsing, he did not wake
Until his wife was stirring.

       Nor till noon
He told her that he'd half a mind to take
His pipes and see if he could turn a tune,
If she would fetch them. And regretfully
She brought the pipes and strapped them on and set
The bellows under his arm, and patiently
She held the reeds to his numb fingers : yet
She knew 'twas worse than useless : Work and years
Had dulled that lively touch ; each joint was stiff
And swollen with rheumatics . . .

      Slowly tears
Ran down his weathered cheeks . . .

       And then a whiff
Of peat-reek filled his nostrils ; and quite still
He sat remembering. Memory was kind
And stripped age off him.

       And along the hill
By Golden Pots he strove against the wind –
In all his days he never again had known

A wind like thon – on that November day.
For every step that he took forward, blown
Half-a-step backward, slowly he made way
Against it, buffeted and battered numb,
Chilled to the marrow, till he reached the door,
To find Jack Dodd, the pitman-piper, come
To play a contest with him . . .
                                        Nevermore
There'd be such piping !
                            Ay, Jack Dodd had heard
That he could play – that up among the hills
There was a lad could pipe like any bird
With half-a-hundred fancy turns and trills,
And give a lead even to Jack himself –
Jack Dodd, the pitmen's champion !
                                        After tea
When they had smoked a while, down from the shelf
He'd reached his own small-pipes, and speedily
They two were at it, playing, tune for tune
Against each other all the winter's night,
And all next morning till the stroke of noon,
Piping out bravely all their hearts' delight.

He still could see Jack, sitting there so lean,
Long-backed, broad-shouldered stooping, and white-faced,
With cropped black head and black eyes burning keen,
Tight-lipped, yet smiling gravely ; round his waist
His small-pipes strapped, the bellows 'neath his arm,
His nimble fingers lively at the reeds –
His body swaying to the lilting charm
Of his own magic piping, till great beads
Of sweat were glistening on his low, white brow.
And he himself, a herd-lad, yellow-haired,
With wide eyes even bluer then than now,
Who sat bolt-upright in his chair and stared
Before him at the steady - glowing peat,
As if each note he played he caught in flight
From the loud wind, and in the quivering heat
Could see it dancing to its own delight.

All night the rafters hummed with piping airs,
And candle and candle guttered out ;
But not a footstep climbed the creaky stairs
To the dark bedrooms. Turn and turn about
They piped or listened : while the wind without
Roared round the steading, battering at the door
As though to burst it wide, then with a shout
Swept on across the pitchy leagues of moor.

Pitman and shepherd piping turn for turn
The airs they loved till to the melody
Their pulses beat ; and their rapt eyes would burn,
Thrilled with the sight that each most loved to see –
The pitman, gazing down a gallery
Of glittering black coal, an endless seam,
As through his piping stole the mystery
Of subterranean waters and of dream
Corridors dwindling everlastingly.

The shepherd, from the top of Windy Gile
Looking o'er range on range of glowing hills,
A world beneath him, stretching, mile on mile,
Brown bent and heather laced by flashing rills –
His body flooded with the light that fills
The veins with running gold -and April light
And wind, and all the melody that spills
From tumbling waters thrilled his pipes that night.

Ay, thon was playing, thon ! And nevermore
The world would hear such piping. Jack was dead.
And he, so old and broken.
                                                    By the door
All day he sat remembering, and in bed
He lay beside his sleeping wife all night
Too spent, too weary, even to toss and turn.
Dawn found him lying, strangely cold and white,
As though still listening to the Otterburn.

DANDY JACK

Whitmonday – he must take the usual stroll
He'd always taken on Bank Holiday
For fifty years or more ; though now that he
Must go alone, it wasn't quite so gay.

Ay, and his clothes, though they were decent black,
And still his best, weren't quite what they had been
When he had donned them first in '87
For the first jubilee of the old Queen –

Not quite so rich a black now, it was true,
And not so suited for festivities –
A trifle shabby at the seams they'd gone,
And shiny at the elbows and the knees.

And he'd always been something of a beau
When he'd strolled at the park at Whitsuntide.
What could he do to smarten himself up ?
Well – it was not so easy to decide.

If he'd had coppers for a buttonhole,
He would have been as happy as a king.
A buttonhole worked wonders . . . Then his eye
Lit on a safety pin – the very thing !

The gilded safety pin that he'd picked up
Last evening in the gutter ; 'twould look gay,
Stuck in the lapel of his coat – ay, ay,
Quite rich and dressy, you might almost say !

With trembling hands he fixed the glittering pin
In his worn broadcloth ; but it shone less bright
Than his black eyes beneath his napless tile
Twinkling with proud and innocent delight.

THE CROWDER

'Twixt Coldmouth Hill and Butterstone Shank
I met an old crowder grizzled and lank,
With his kit tucked under his arm,
And I called to him, *"Crowder, whither away ?"*
And he answered : *"I'm due upon Michaelmas Day*
To fiddle at Cherrytree's Farm –
For I play 'Bobbie Shafto' and 'Stagshaw Bank Fair',
'The Waters of Tyne', 'Elsie Marley',
'Chevy Chase' and the 'Keel Row' and
'Dick o' the Cow,'
and 'Over the Water to Charlie !'"

And I called to him : *"Crowder, come fiddle away !*
For it's well-nigh a week until Michaelmas Day,
And I'll dance till you've a crick in your arm –
A crick in your arm and a crick in your back,
And your fiddle-strings snap and your fiddle
bridge crack –
Then heigh-ho ! for Cherrytree's Farm –
For I dance 'Bobbie Shafto' and 'Stagshaw Bank Fair',
'The Waters of Tyne', 'Elsie Marley'
'Chevy Chase' and the 'Keel Row' and
'Dick o' the Cow,'
and 'Over the Water to Charlie !'"

And he up with his kit and he fiddled away,
And I danced to his fiddling till Michaelmas Day –
And never a crick in his arm !
Then he held out his hat, and the devil to pay,
As I sat in the ditch, and he wished me *"Good Day",*
And hurried to Cherrytree's Farm,
To play *'Bobbie Stafto' and 'Stagshaw Bank Fair'.*
'The Waters of Tyne', 'Elsie Marley'
'Chevy Chase' and the 'Keel Row' and
'Dick o' the Cow,'
And 'Over the Water to Charlie !'

BESSIE STOKOE

He stood with the other young herds
At the Hiring to-day :
And I laughed and I chaffed and changed words
With every young hind of them all
As I stopped by the lollipop stall,
But never a word did he say.

He had straggly long straw-coloured hair
And a beard like a goat –
In his breeches a badly-stitched tear
That I longed, standing there in the crush,
To re-mend, as I hankered to brush
The ruddle and fluff from his coat.

But his bonnie blue eyes staring wide
Looked far beyond me,
As though on some distant fellside
His dogs were collecting the sheep,
And he anxiously watched them to keep
A young dog from running too free –

And I almost expected to hear
From the lips of the lad
A shrill whistle sing in my ear,
As he eyed that green hillside, to check
The fussy black frolicking speck
From chasing the grey specks like mad . . .

So I left them and went on my way
With a lad with black hair ;
And we swung and rode round all the day
To the racket of corncrake and gong ;
But I never forgot in the throng
The lad with the far-away stare.

The jimmy-smart groom at my side
Had twinkling black eyes ;
But the grin on his mouth was too wide,
And his hands with my hands were too free :

So I took care to slip him at tea
As he turned round to pay for the pies :

And I left him alone on the seat
With the teapot and cups,
And the two pies he'd paid for to eat.
If he happens to think of the cause,
It may teach him to keep his red paws
For the handling of horses and pups.

But alone in the rain and the dark,
As I made for the farm,
I halted a moment to hark
To the sound of a shepherd's long stride,
And the shy lad stepped up to my side
And I felt his arm link through my arm.

So it seems after all I'm to mend
Those breeches, and keep
That shaggy head clipped to the end,
And the shaggy chin clean, and to give
That coat a good brush – and to live
All my days in the odour of sheep.

SAM HOGARTH

He sits – his open Bible on his knee,
Nell, his old whippet, curled up at his feet –
Muttering at whiles and nodding drowsily
Over the damped slack-fire that dully burns
In the little grate : then shifting in his seat
He lifts the book with shaky hands, his head
Wagging with eagerness, and, fumbling, turns
From the tenth chapter of Genesis, unread,
To the well-thumbed flyleaf at the back, to pore
With spectacled, weak, reverent eyes once more,
Lest it escape his failing memory,
On Nell's proud scrawl-recorded pedigree.

OLD MEG

There's never the taste of a cherry for me,
They're out of my reach on the bough,
And it's hard to be seeing them hang on the tree –
And no man to hand me them now.

It's hard to be travelling since Billy Boy died,
With the devil's own crick in my back,
With the gout in my knees and a stitch in my side –
And no man to carry my pack.

It's hard to be travelling the roads all alone,
When cherries hang handy and ripe –
And no man to find me a soft mossy stone,
And no man to kindle my pipe.

ELLEN CHESTER

After working all day at the tan-pits,
With strong hands tanned horny and hard
And stained with the bark brown as leather,
He would come every day from the yard ;

And I, from my work at the laundry,
With hands soused in suds clean and white
And soft to the touch as old linen,
Would meet him half-way every night :

Would meet him half-way every evening,
Though always I shuddered to feel
Those hard fingers gripping my fingers
And crushing my soft hands like steel.

But now I'm forgot and forsaken ;
And eagerly waiting he stands
For a girl coming from the gardens
With weathered and grubby red hands.

41

As unseen in the dark of a doorway
I watch him alone and apart,
My cold fingers fumble my bosom
To loosen his clutch from my heart.

BETTY RIDDLE

As she sits at her stall in the Martinmas Fair
With a patched blue umbrella slung over her chair.
Old Betty Riddle sells
Greenjacks and jargonels,
Fixing some ghost of old days with her stare.

"A ha'p'orth of greenjacks !" each little boy cries,
Devouring six-penn'orth at least with his eyes :
Into his grubby hands
Pears drop as still he stands ;
But she gives him no glance as he munches his prize.

While mumbling and mowing she sits all the day,
And her mellow green pyramids dwindle away,
Folk in the roundabout
Racket and skirl and shout ;
Yet never a word to it all does she say.

And even if, when her whole stock-in-trade's bought,
Some laughing lad's eye by that cold stare is caught,
Glumly away he'll slink
Too dull of wit to think
Of offering a penny to her for her thought.

THE ICE

Her day out from the workhouse-ward, she stands,
A grey-haired woman decent and precise,
With prim black bonnet and neat paisley shawl,
Among the other children by the stall,
And with grave relish eats a penny ice.

To wizened toothless gums with quaking hands
She holds it, shuddering with delicious cold,
Nor heeds the jeering laughter of young men –
The happiest, in her innocence, of all :
For, while their insolent youth must soon grow old,
She, who's been old, is now a child again.

SALLY BLACK AND GEORDIE GREEN

Oh, where may you be going with your black mare sleeked so shinily,
With her four hoofs newly-varnished and her feathers combed so clean,
With her mane and tail straw-plaited, pranked so gay and smart and nattily
With red and yellow ribbons tied in lovelocks, Geordie Green ?
I be going to the Fair
With my mare.

Then won't you take me with you, for I've never been to Stagshaw Bank,
Nor a hiring nor a hopping, though I'm nearly seventeen,
And I've never had a fairing, faldalal nor whigmaleerie nor
A red and yellow ribbon for my lovelocks, Geordie Green ?
I can't manage but one mare
At the Fair.

Now what can you be fearing, and I but a young lassie, too,
And you, a lad of twenty ? But if so it be you're mean,
I've saved up thirteen pennies, so no need to fear I'll beggar you
Or be beholding to you for one farthing, Geordie Green.
I'll be getting to the Fair
With my mare.

Then gan your gait and luck to you at Stagshaw Bank, your mare and you ;
But maybe you'll be rueing when you see me like a queen
In Farmer Dodd's new dogcart, with the shafts and spokes picked out
with red,
Overtake you on the road there and flash by you, Geordie Green.
Yet I'll happen reach the Fair
With my mare.

NED NIXON AND HIS MAGGIE

Will you come with me, Maggie, to Stagshaw Bank Fair ?
Come with you where – come with you where ?
Do you fancy a lass has naught better to do
Than to go gallivanting, Ned Nixon, with you ?

If you come with me, Maggie, I'll buy you a ring.
You'll do no such thing – you'll do no such thing.
Do you fancy I'd let my lad squander his pence
On tokens and trinkets and such-like nonsense ?

Come, Maggie, come, Maggie, we're only once young !
Now hold your fool's tongue – now hold your fool's
                                                                    tongue !
If we're only young once it behoves us to be
A common-sense couple and act cannily.

Time enough, Maggie, for sense when we're old.
Does copper turn gold – does copper turn gold,
Or a guff turn wiseacre at three-score-and ten ?
Anyhow, I'm for taking no chances with men.

Then must I go lonesome to Stagshaw Bank Fair ?
What do I care – what do I care ?
But if you go lonesome I'd have you to know
It's lonesome the rest of your life you will go.

44

THE BEARERS

So, you're all there ! I fancied I'd have lived
To act as bearer to the lot of you –
Tom Dodd, Dick Dobson, Jacob Hetherington,
Mick Hall, Dan Lishman and Nick Ingledew :
So, you're all there, my hearties ! And me here . . .
Well, I must say, you're six good lads and true !

Good lads and true are you to shoulder me
On the last jaunt I'll ever take with you –
Tom Dodd, Dick Dobson, Jacob Hetherington,
Mick Hall, Dan Lishman and Nick Ingledew.
Now, keep in step ; and, when your own time comes,
May you be borne by lads as good and true.

THE IMMORTAL

Writhen and grey as an old shank of heather,
Tending his flock, I met John Armitage,
Who bleated at me like an old bell-wether –
Your grandfather and I were of an age.

Though through my very bones the snell wind whistled,
Or, so it seemed, on that storm-scoured fell,
Still those old toothless jaws, so lank and grizzled,
Piped – *And your father, too, I knew him well.*

And, as he talked, the life within me dwindled . . .
And I, the wraith of one whose day was done,
Stood watching him, still hale, with blue eyes kindled,
Telling the same tale to my unborn son.

THE BARLEY MOW

Snug on the settles of the Barley Mow
The village elders in the warmth and light
Over their glasses gossip, while the night
Against the blacked-out casement slashes snow
In gust on gust of fury – relishing
In ancient bones the pleasant tingling glow,
They gossip ; and yet every now and then
They pause, embarrassed, as though pondering,
While icy silence in the taproom falls,
Some curious lack ; and only vaguely know
Their old hearts tarry in the intervals
For the light laughter and the bantering
Of the absent voices of the younger men.

THE WHITE WHIPPET

Squatted on their hunkers at the corner of the street
Outside the Pouter Pigeon a knot of pitmen sat
Waiting for the doors to open, cursing the raw sleet,
Or muttering with husky throats dully of this and that :

When suddenly within the ring of the street-lamp's gusty flame,
Out of the stormy shadows of the black November night,
Like a little slip of moonshine a snow-white whippet came
And stayed one breathless moment before their startled sight.

Speechless they gazed upon her as she stood with lifted paw,
Clean-limbed, with quivering muzzle and jetty eyes agleam,
Nor heard the doors swing open wide as each lad looked with awe
One moment on the vision of his own heart's secret dream.

SARAH

Let us with a cheerful mind
Praise the lord, for He is kind –

No one at all to talk to through the week,
And nobody to answer, should she speak –
In her old outby cottage all alone
Lives Sarah, mute as her own threshold stone ;
And all day long keeps turning in her head,
Like a trapped mouse, some thing she might have said.
If only anyone who cared to hear
What she was thinking ever should come near.
So, like the stopped clock on the mantelshelf,
She lives her life, shut up within herself
Six days a week, till Sunday comes, when she,
In the back pew beneath the gallery,
As the whole village joins with one accord,
Lets herself go in singing to the Lord –

And His mercy shall endure,
Ever faithful, ever sure.

HER EPITAPH

Weep not for me, my friends so dear, for I am only gone to see
That precious house my dearest Lord is furnishing for me.

Dear Betsy Brown, remembering how all
Your chairs and tables shone with such a gloss –
They seemed to smile a welcome – I feel sure
You chose the verse that's cut upon your cross :
For in a heaven without furniture
To polish you'd be sorely at a loss ;
And your idea of paradise would be
A mansion furnished in mahogany
To be spring-cleaned throughout eternity.

THE HUMAN CANNON-BALL

Being a human cannon-ball don't take up all your time –
And few the turns I couldn't do when I was in my prime ;
But now the folk I talk to seem to marvel most of all
To think old Dolly Dobbs was once a human cannon-ball.

'Twas only for a year or two, and then just twice a day,
And circus-bred-and-born, to me 'twas nothing out of the way :
I couldn't stand it now of course, with aches and pains and all ;
But where's the young wench wouldn't be a human cannon-ball ?

Tough, mind you, I'm not saying that I shall ever forget
How dizzy-like I felt when first I landed in the net ;
But, sure, the jolts life gives you, not expecting them at all,
Upset you ten times worse than being a human cannon-ball.

I'd never think to mention it, if I could have my way ;
But then folks won't listen to what else I've got to say :
That I'm the mother of six sons don't interest at all
The fools that gape to hear about the human cannon-ball.

VENUS DI MILO

The gipsy mother could afford no stone,
Her little lassie's nameless grave to mark,
Her baby Nita, lying there alone,
Lapped in the old earth's bosom, cold and dark.

But one day in an old-junkshop she found,
And bought with her last pence, a statuette :
And so, returning to the burial-ground
Upon the tiny new-made grave she set

Venus di Milo : and still love's high Queen,
Born of the beauty of the breaking wave,
In marble immortality serene
Keeps vigil o'er the gipsy baby's grave.

DEAR, OH DEAR !

It's lone work going to the Fair without a lad ;
But never in my lifetime a lover have I had :
And yet a fair's a fair ; and how should I stop away,
When all the folk are going there on Michaelmas Day.
But never has a lad of them called me his "dear" ;
And now I'm getting on, and over old, I fear :
For I've never been any man's dear, Oh dear !
Though now I'm nearly into my seventeenth year.

All the lads and lasses went linking on their way
About me to the Fair ; and their hearts were light and gay :
But my heart was sad and lonely, as I strolled about the Fair,
With not a lad for my lad of all the lads there.
It's true the wheedling cheapjacks called me their "dear" ;
But none of them was meaning it, that I sadly fear :
For I've never been any man's dear, Oh dear !
Thought now I'm nearly into my seventeenth year.

And, as I strolled about, a Jill without a Jack,
I couldn't bear the lonesomeness ; and so I came back :
And I don't fancy going any more to the Fair ;
And if I stop away – why, there's nobody to care :
For never has a lad of them called me his "dear" ;
And now I'm getting on, and over old, I fear :
For I've never been any man's dear, Oh dear !
And a maid's an old maid in her seventeenth year.

WORKING LIFE

GOLD

All day the mallet thudded, far below
My garret, in an old ramshackle shed
Where, ceaselessly, with stiffly nodding head
And rigid motions ever to and fro,
A figure like a puppet in a show
Before the window moved till day was dead,
Beating out gold to earn his daily bread,
Beating out thin fine gold-leaf blow on blow.

And I within my garret all day long
To that unceasing thudding tuned my song,
Beating out golden words in tune and time
To that dull thudding, rhyme on golden rhyme :
But in my dreams all night in that dark shed
With aching arms I beat fine gold for bread.

THE PAISLEY SHAWL

What were his dreams who wove this coloured shawl –
The grey hard-bitten weaver gaunt and dour
Out of whose grizzled memory, even as a flower
Out of bleak winter at young April's call
In the old tradition of flowers breaks into bloom,
Blossomed the ancient intricate design
Of softly-glowing hues and exquisite line –
What were his dreams, crouched at his cottage-loom ?

What were her dreams, the laughing April lass,
Who first, in the flowering of young delight
With parted lips and eager tilted head
And shining eyes, about her shoulders white
Drew the soft fabric of kindling green and red,
Before her candle-lighted looking-glass ?

THE HAPPY WAY

The pithead lowers black
Against the rainy grey,
As down the cinder-track
They take their happy way –

He, cracking all the while
Of his white whippet, Nell :
She, listening with a smile
To all he has to tell.

Happy to hear him talk,
As he, to have her by,
Light-heartedly they walk
Beneath the heavy sky.

For them no turning back,
Though not a word they say
Of love, as down the track
They take their happy way.

THE PONIES

During the strike, the ponies were brought up
From their snug stables, some three hundred feet
Below the surface – up the pit's main shaft
Shot one by one into the light of day:
And as each stepped, bewildered, from the cage,
He stood amongst his fellows, shivering
In the unaccustomed freshness of free air,
His dim eyes dazzled by the April light.
And then one suddenly left the huddled group,
Lifted his muzzle, snuffed the freshness in,
Pawed the soft turf and, whinnying, started trotting
Across the field; and one by one his fellows
With pricking ears each slowly followed him,
Timidly trotting: when the leader's trot
Broke into a canter, then into a gallop;
And now the whole herd galloped at his heels
Around the dewy meadow, hard hoofs, used

To stumble over treacherous stony tramways
And plunging hock-deep through the black steamy
puddles
Of the dusky narrow galleries, delighting
In the soft spring of the resilient turf.
Still round and round the field they raced, unchecked
By tugging traces, at their heels no longer
The trundling tubs, and round and round,
With a soft thunder of hoofs, the sunshine flashing
On their sleek coats, through the bright April weather
They raced all day; and even when the night
Kindled clear stars above them in the sky
Strangely unsullied by the stack which now
No longer belched out blackness, still they raced,
Unwearied, as though their short sturdy limbs
The rebel blood like wildfire ran, their lungs
Filled with the breath of freedom. On they sped
Through the sweet dewy darkness; and all night
The watchman at the pithead heard the thudding
Of the careering and exultant hoofs
Still circling in a crazy chase; and dawn
Found them still streaming raggedly around,
Tailing into a lagging cantering,
And so to a stumbling trot; when gradually,
Dropping out one by one, they started cropping
The dew-dank tender grass, which no foul reek
From the long idle pit now smirched, and drinking
With quivering nostrils the rich living breath
Of sappy growing things, the cool rank green
Grateful to eyes, familiar from their colthood
Only with darkness and the dusty glimmer
Of lamplit galleries . . .

                  Mayhap one day
Our masters, too, will go on strike, and we
Escape the dark and drudgery of the pit,
And race unreined around the fields of heaven!

Plate 1 (right)

Portrait of Wilfrid Gibson by
photographer Sherrill Schell c.1913

Plate 2 (below)

Wilfrid Wilson Gibson was born on
2nd October 1878 in Hexham,
Northumberland; his family home
was at 1 Battle Hill Terrace, seen
here in the centre of this early
20th century photograph taken by
his father John Pattison Gibson.

Plate 3
The Old Nail Shop, Dymock, Gloucestershire:
The home of Wilfrid and Geraldine Gibson c.1913

Plate 4   Wilfrid at Dymock c.1913

Plates 5 & 6
Interior photographs,
taken by Wilfrid, of the
Old Nail Shop.

Plate 7 -Wilfrid and Michael Gibson at sea 1929

Below Plate 8 - Flannan Isle Lighthouse c.1900 — see page 61

The lighthouse, built in late 1890s, stands on Eilean Mor – one of the remote Flannan Isles off the west coast of Scotland. Gibson's poem, written in 1912, is based on a true event dating from December 1900, when three lighthouse keepers, James Ducat, Thomas Marshall and Donald MacArthur, vanished without trace from the lighthouse.

AT THE PIT-HEAD

Black was his face
With the dust of the pit,
But bright as hot coals
His eyes burned in it

The first time I felt
His gaze fixed on me,
And wondering turned
Half-frightened to see

The fire of his heart
That paled the sunshine
Blazing out of the eyes
That looked into mine

Till an answering flame
In my bosom was lit
By those eyes burning out
From the mirk of the pit.

THE COUNTERPANE

The buzzer is sounding again ;
And the lads, trooping by through the rain :
Yet I only snuggle the closer
Under the patched counterpane.

I made it, myself, for the bed,
Every stitch of it, when we were wed :
– A gaudy loud quilt to lie under !
'Twould keep him awake – Robert said.

But that was his joke : he would sleep
So soundly, he often would keep
Me awake half the night with his snoring,
Till I was nigh ready to weep.

He sleeps soundly now – but it's white,
The quilt that's his covering to-night ;
While I, all alone 'neath the patchwork,
Lie 'waiting the blink of daylight.

And now the pit's working again :
And some other lad troops through the rain
To take Robert's shift, while I snuggle
Under the patched counterpane.

HEWER OF WOOD

The timber I have hewn, stacked high,
Would overtop Saint Mary's spire
That soars into the windy sky,
Yet it has only served for fuel
To feed one little cottage-fire –

Has only served to keep aglow
One inglenook when winter's storm
Raked heaven and earth with blinding snow –
A forest felled and life-long labour
To keep a little household warm.

And that small fire that still devours
Fresh timber burns my life away :
The tale of gold and glooming hours
Of tree and man's the selfsame story –
Green flame, red flame and ashes grey.

THE GOOD NEWS

Cutting an iron plate with a cold-chisel,
His hammer's stunning clang
Through all the workshop rang,
As I stept in out of the seeping drizzle :

And, even as I stood behind him, laughing,
With all his mind intent,
And his whole being bent
On cutting the tough metal, till the chaffing

Of laughing mates rang louder in his hearing,
He worked, nor turned to see :
But, when he looked at me,
And read my eyes' good news – at one leap clearing

The crowded workshop, clutching still his chisel,
Home to his wife he ran –
Home, like a crazy man,
The happy father ran through the cold drizzle.

THE RELEASE

All day he shoves the pasteboard in
The slick machine that turns out boxes,
A box a minute ; and its din
Is all his music, as he stands
And feeds it ; while his jaded brain
Moves only out and in again
With the slick motion of his hands,
Monotonously making boxes,
A box a minute – all his thoughts
A slick succession of empty boxes.

But, when night comes, and he is free
To play his fiddle, with the music
His whole soul moves to melody ;
No more recalling day's dumb round,
His reckless spirit sweeps and whirls
On surging waves and dizzy swirls
And eddies of enchanted sound ;
And in a flame-winged flight of music
Above the roofs and chimneys soars
To ride the starry tides of music.

UNDER THE SHAWL

She happed her shawl about her head ;
And clattered quickly down the hill,
Among the other hands who trudged
With clacking clogs towards the mill.

From other shawls, young voices called,
With laughing words and quick replies :
And, now and then, the dawning light
Showed a bright glint of teeth and eyes.

But not a word for anyone
Had she ; nor did she lift her head
To greet the light : but brooded still,
Within her shawl, on what he'd said –

Those fatal words that, though he'd tried,
Ashamed too late, to take them back,
In the dark hollow of her brain
Kept clacking with the clogs' clack-clack.

THE OLD NAIL-SHOP

I dreamt of wings – and waked to hear
Through the low-sloping ceiling clear
The nesting starlings flutter and scratch
Among the rafters of the thatch,
Not twenty inches from my head ;
And lay, half dreaming in my bed,
Watching the far elms – bolt-upright,
Black towers of silence in a night
Of stars – between the window-sill
And the low-hung eaves, square-framed, until
I drowsed, and must have slept a wink . . .
And wakened to a ceaseless clink
Of hammers ringing on the air . . .
And, somehow, only half aware,
I'd risen and crept down the stair,
Bewildered by strange, smoky gloom,

Until I'd reached the living-room
That once had been a nail-shop shed.
And where my hearth had blazed, instead
I saw the nail-forge glowing red ;
And, through the stife and smoky glare,
Three dreaming women standing there
With hammers beating red-hot wire
On tinkling anvils, by the fire,
To ten-a-penny nails ; and heard –
Though none looked up or breathed a word –
The song each heart sang to the tune
Of hammers, through a summer's noon,
When they had wrought in that red glow,
Alive, a hundred years ago –
The song of girl and wife and crone,
Sung in the heart of each alone . . .

The dim-eyed crone with nodding head –
"He's dead ; and I'll, too, soon be dead"

The grave-eyed mother, gaunt with need –
"Another little mouth to feed !"

The black-eyed girl, with eyes alight –
"I'll wear the yellow beads to-night."

JANUARY NIGHTFALL

A scintillating snake of jewelled light
Kindles the darkness as from forge and mill,
Free-wheeling gaily down the Letchworth hill,
The workers hurry home through early night.
Beneath the frosty stars, an endless stream,
One after one the little lamps shoot down
The long and gradual slope to Hitchin town ;
And happy voices call and faces gleam
Suddenly from the shadows, as they pass –
Lasses and lads released from bench and loom,
From clanging foundry and from rattling room
Where all day long beneath the roof of glass

On whirring wheels the live belts strain and scream –
Released at last, for a few hours to be
Masters of their own time, a brief while free
To call the tune and dance, or drowse and dream.

THE CHEERFUL SWEEP

From the deep pit of sleep
I rose, disgruntled, to let in the sweep
Who rattled loudly at the kitchen door :
And shuffling, slippered, down the stair,
Shivering in the nippy air,
Switched on the light
And turned the key,
And standing there,
His black face gleaming in the glare
Against the tardy tarrying winter night :
When through the grime his smile broke merrily
As sunshine through a thundercloud, and he
Wished me "Good morning !"
                                        Back to bed I crept,
To snuggle once again
Beneath the counterpane
Among warm cosy blankets, while he swept :
And as I lay
Awaiting day,
I wondered, if it had devolved on me,
The job of sweeping others' chimneys clean,
So that their hearth fires might burn cheerily,
If ever I had been
So single-hearted that all men might see
Through soot and grime the flame of life in me
Burning with such a crystal clarity.

MYSTERY AND IMAGINATION

THE DANCING SEAL

When we were building Skua Light –
The first men who had lived a night
Upon that deep-sea Isle –
As soon as chisel touched the stone,
The friendly seals would come ashore ;
And sit and watch us all the while,
As though they'd not seen men before ;
And so, poor beasts, had never known
Men had the heart to do them harm.
They'd little cause to feel alarm
With us, for we were glad to find
Some friendliness in that strange sea ;
Only too pleased to let them be
And sit as long as they'd a mind
To watch us : for their eyes were kind
Like women's eyes, it seemed to me,
So, hour on hour, they sat : I think
They liked to hear the chisels' clink :
And when the boy sang loud and clear,
They scrambled closer in to hear ;
And if he whistled sweet and shrill,
The queer beasts shuffled nearer still :
But every sleek and sheeny skin
Was mad to hear his violin.

When, work all over for the day,
He'd take his fiddle down and play
His merry tunes beside the sea,
Their eyes grew brighter and more bright,
And burned and twinkled merrily :
And as I watched them one still night,
And saw their eager sparkling eyes,
I felt those lively seals would rise
Some shiny night ere he could know,
And dance about him, heel and toe,
Unto the fiddle's heady tune.

And at the rising of the moon,
Half-daft, I took my stand before
A young seal lying on the shore ;
And called on her to dance with me.
And it seemed hardly strange when she
Stood up before me suddenly,
And shed her black and sheeny skin ;
And smiled, all eager to begin . . .
And I was dancing, heel and toe,
With a young maiden white as snow,
Unto a crazy violin.

We danced beneath the dancing moon
All night beside the dancing sea
With tripping toes and skipping heals,
And all about us friendly seals
Like Christian folk were dancing reels
Unto the fiddle's endless tune
That kept on spinning merrily
As though it never meant to stop ;
And never once the snow-white maid
A moment stayed
To take a breath,
Though I was fit to drop ;
And while those wild eyes challenged me
I knew as well as well could be
I must keep step with that young girl,
Though we should dance to death.

Then with a skirl
The fiddle broke :
The moon went out :
The sea stopped dead :
And in a twinkling all the rout
Of dancing fold had fled ….
And in the chill bleak dawn I woke
Upon the naked rock alone.

They've brought me far from Skua Isle …
I laugh to think they do not know
That, as all day I chip the stone

Among my fellow here inland,
I smell the sea-wrack on the shore …
And see her snowy tossing hand,
And meet again her merry smile …
And dream I'm dancing all the while,
I'm dancing ever, heel and toe,
With a seal-maiden white as snow,
On that moonshiny island-strand
For ever and for evermore.

FLANNAN ISLE

"Though three men dwell on Flannan Isle
To keep the lamp alight,
As we steered under the lee, we caught
No glimmer through the night."

A passing ship at dawn had brought
The news ; and quickly we set sail,
To find out what strange thing might ail
The keepers of the deep-sea light.

The Winter day broke blue and bright,
With glancing sun and glancing spray,
While o'er the swell our boat made way,
As gallant as a gull in flight.

But as we neared the lonely Isle,
And looked up at the naked height,
And saw the lighthouse towering white,
With blinded lantern, that all night
Had never shot a spark
Of comfort through the dark,
So ghostly in the cold sunlight
It seemed, that we were struck the while
With wonder all too dread for words.

And as into the tiny creek
We stole beneath the hanging crag,
We saw three queer, black, ugly birds –
Too big, by far, in my belief,

For cormorant or shag –
Like seamen sitting bolt-upright
Upon a half-tide reef :
But, as we neared, they plunged from sight,
Without a sound, or spurt of white.

And still too mazed to speak,
We landed ; and made fast the boat ;
And climbed the track in single file,
Each wishing he were safe afloat,
On any sea, however far,
So it be far from Flannan Isle :
And still we seemed to climb, and climb,
As though we'd lost all count of time,
And so must climb for evermore.
Yet, all too soon, we reached the door –
The black, sun-blistered lighthouse-door,
That gaped for us ajar.

As, on the threshold, for a spell,
We paused, we seemed to breathe the smell
Of limewash and of tar,
Familiar as our daily breath,
As though 'twere some strange scent of death :
And so, yet wondering, side by side,
We stood a moment, still tongue-tied :
And each with black foreboding eyed
The door, ere we should fling it wide,
To leave the sunlight for the gloom :
Till, plucking courage up, at last,
Hard on each other's heels we passed,
Into the living-room.

Yet, as we crowded through the door,
We only saw a table, spread
For dinner, meat and cheese and bread ;

But all untouched ; and no one there :
As though, when they sat down to eat,
Ere they could even taste,
Alarm had come ; and they in haste
Had risen and left the bread and meat :

For at the table-head a chair
Lay tumbled on the floor.

We listened ; but we only heard
The feeble cheeping of a bird
That starved upon its perch :
And, listening still, without a word,
We set about our hopeless search.

We hunted high, we hunted low ;
And soon ransacked the empty house ;
Then o'er the Island, to and fro,
We ranged, to listen and to look
In every cranny, cleft or nook.
That might have hid a bird or mouse :
But, though we searched from shore to shore,
We found no sign in any place :
And soon again stood face to face
Before the gaping door :
And stole into the room once more
As frightened children steal.
Ay : though we hunted high and low,
And hunted everywhere,
Of the three men's fate we found no trace
Of any kind in any place,
But a door ajar, and an untouched meal
And an overtoppled chair.

And as we listened in the gloom
Of that forsaken living-room –
A chill clutch on our breath –
We thought how ill-chance came to all
Who kept the Flannan Light :
And how the rock had been the death
Of many a likely lad :
How six had come to a sudden end,
And three had gone stark mad :
And one whom we'd all known as friend
Had leapt from the lantern one still night,
And fallen dead by the lighthouse wall :
And long we thought

On the three we sought,
And of what might yet befall.

Like curs a glance has brought to heel,
We listened, flinching there :
And looked, and looked, on the untouched meal,
And the overtoppled chair

We seemed to stand for an endless while,
Though still no word was said,
Three men, alive on Flannan Isle,
Who thought on three men dead.

THE VIXEN

The vixen made for Deadman's Flow,
Where not a mare but mine could go :
And three hounds only splashed across
The quaking hags of mile-wide moss ;
Only three of the deadbeat pack
Scrambled out by Lone Maid's Slack,
Bolter, Tough, and Ne'er-die-Nell :
But as they broke across the fell
The tongue they gave was good to hear,
 Lively music clean and clear,
Such as only light-coats make,
Hot-trod through the girth-deep brake.

The vixen, draggled and nigh spent,
Twisted through the rimy bent
Towards the Christhope Crags. I thought
Every earth stopt . . . winded . . . caught . . .
She's a mask and brush ! When white
A squall of snow swept all from sight ;

And hoodman-blind, Lightfoot and I,
Battled with the roaring sky.

When southerly the snow had swept,
Light broke, as the vixen crept
Slinking up the stony brae.

On a jutting scar she lay,
Panting, lathered, while she eyed
The hounds that took the stiff brae-side
With yelping music, mad to kill.

Then vixen, hounds and craggy hill
Were smothered in a blinding swirl :
And when it passed, there stood a girl
Where the vixen late had lain,
Smiling down as I drew rein,
Baffled ; and the hounds, deadbeat,
Fawning at the young girl's feet,
Whimpered, cowed, where her red hair,
Streaming to her ankles bare,
Turned as white among the heather
As the vixen's brush's feather.

Flinching on my flinching mare,
I watched her, gaping and astare,
As she smiled with red lips wide,
White fangs curving either side
Of her lolling tongue . . . My thrapple
Felt fear's fang : I strove, agrapple,
Reeling . . . and again blind snow
Closed like night.
                              No man may know
How Lightfoot won through Deadman's Flow.
And naught I knew till, in the glow
Of home's wide door, my wife's kind face
Smiled welcome. And for me the chase,
The last chase, ended. Though the pack
Through the blizzard struggled back,
Gone were Bolter, Tough, and Nell,
Where, the vixen's self can tell !
Long we sought them, high and low,
By Christhope Crag and Deadman's Flow,
By slack and syke and hag : and found
Never bone nor hair of hound.

THE ICE-CART

Perched on my city office-stool
I watched with envy while a cool
And lucky carter handled ice . . .
And I was wandering in a trice
Far from the grey and grimy heat
Of that intolerable street
O'er sapphire berg and emerald floe
Beneath the still cold ruby glow
Of everlasting Polar night,
Bewildered by the queer half-light,
Until I stumbled unawares
Upon a creek where big white bears
Plunged headlong down with flourished heels
And floundered after shining seals
Through shivering seas of blinding blue.
And, as I watched them, ere I knew
I'd stripped and I was swimming too
Among the seal-pack, young and hale,
And thrusting on with threshing tail,
With twist and twirl and sudden leap
Through crackling ice and salty deep,
Diving and doubling with my kind
Until at last we left behind
Those big white blundering bulks of death,
And lay at length with panting breath
Upon a far untravelled floe
Beneath a gentle drift of snow –
Snow drifting gently, fine and white
Out of the endless Polar night,
Falling and falling evermore
Upon that far untravelled shore
Till I was buried fathoms deep
Beneath the cold white drifting sleep –

Sleep drifting deep,
Deep drifting sleep . . .

The carter cracked a sudden whip :
I clutched my stool with startled grip,
Awakening to the grimy heat
Of that intolerable street.

THE LONELY INN

He comes at dusk to the lonely inn ;
And the crazy door swings wide,
As he wearily lifts the noiseless latch,
And steps inside.

But no one greets him, as he steps
From the dusk to a deeper gloom ;
And not a glint of light steals out
From any room.

Sore, on his weary way, he's longed
To sit by a friendly fire :
But an empty grate and a stone-cold hearth
Chill his desire.

As, quaking there, he knows at last
That he is only a ghost
Who has come to dwell at the lonely inn,
With death for host.

THE OLD WIFE

The cold rain, seeping through the rotten thatch,
Drips on the floor ;
And squalling winds that bluster at the door
Rattle the latch.

Beside the chilly hearth the old wife sits
With nodding head,
As a faint gleam comes from the days long dead
To failing wits –

And snug and warm beneath the cosy thatch,
She dreams once more,
Happy to hear a loved hand at the door
Lifting the latch.

THE RIDER OF THE WHITE HORSE

Climbing the bridge's slope, a little lad,
I looked up and beheld in bright sunlight,
Against a billowing April cloud, blue-black,
Heavy with threat of hail, a monster white
High-stepping steed with rider scarlet-clad
Like a flame-robed archangel on its back.

The spark-red nostril and the flashing eye,
The scarlet rider in the sun afire
Against the storm-cloud – shot with thrilling dread
My little heart, a-hunger with desire
Of angel visions : then, as they went by,
I knew 'twas old Jake Dodd in hunting red –

Jake Dodd, the whipper-in, on his white Jill.
The sun was blotted out ; the hail threshed down,
Scattering the glory. Jake and his old mare
Have long been dust – yet, on the bridge's crown,
In the child's heart within my heart, Jake still
Rides, an archangel burning through the air.

WATER FROM THE HILLS

He clangs the furnace-door
On the heat and glare are roar,
And wipes his brow ; and, tilting
The bucket, takes a pull
At waters sweet and cool ;
And, as he drinks, it seems to him
That he is home once more.

For the water, drawn so far
From the springs by Eagle Scar,
Has a smack of peat about it ;
And he seems to drink the cool
Waters of the amber pool
Underneath the granite boulder,
All aglint with flakes of spar.

On his belly in the ling,
Gazing deep into the spring,
With his lips to welling waters
Once again he seems to lie
Underneath the April sky,
So alive with skylarks singing
That it seems, itself, to sing.

THE UNSEEN RIDER

The road blocked deep with drifts, when Helen died,
We had to cross the fells, scoured clean of snow,
To reach the little churchyard in the dale,
Her coffin strapped across the saddlebow
Of her young chestnut filly, Heatherbell,
Bridling and restive under the deadweight
Of that strange burden ; when down Elkridgeside
There swirled a scathing blast of blinding hail ;
And the young lad who held the bridle-rein,
Stumbling among the tussocks, slipped and fell ;
And Heatherbell broke loose and plunged and reared ;
Then, as the scared lad snatched at her in vain,
She dashed across the fell and disappeared
In the dense flurry of the squall : too late
We cantered after her ; and never again
Was she or the dread burden that she bore
Seen by a living soul. Yet oft at night
The muffled drumming hoofs of Heatherbell
Are heard by lonely shepherds on the fell
As, high of heart as she would ride of old,
Helen, who that wild day in death's despite
Escaped the durance of the churchyard mould,
Ranges the fells she loved for evermore.

NATURE AND COUNTRYSIDE

THE LAMBING

Softly she slept in the night – her newborn bairn at her breast,
A wee warm crinkled hand to the dimpling bosom pressed –
As I rose from her side to go, though sore was my heart to stay,
To the ease of the labouring ewes that else would have died before day.

Banking the peats on the hearth, I reached from the rafter-hook
My lanthorn and kindled the wick ; and taking my plaid and my crook,
I lifted the latch and turned once more to see if she slept ;
And looked on the slumber of peace ere into the night I stepped –

Into the swirling dark of the driving, blinding sleet,
And a world that seemed to sway and slip from under my feet
As if rocked in the wind that swept the starless roaring night,
Yet fumed in a fury vain at my lanthorn's shielded light.

Clean-drenched in the first wild gust I battled across the garth
And passed through the clashing gate – the warm peat-glow of the hearth
And the quiet of love in my breast, the craven voices to quell,
As I set my teeth to the wind and turned to the open fell.

Over the tussocky bent I strove till I reached the fold –
My brow like ice and my hands so numbed that they scarce could hold
My crook or unloosen the pen ; but I heard a lamb's weak cries
As the gleam of my lanthorn lit the night of its newborn eyes.

Toiling and trembling I watched each young life struggle for breath –
Fighting till dawn for my flock with the oldest of herdsmen, death ;
And glad was my heart when at last the stackyard again I crossed,
And thought of the labour well-over with never a yeanling lost.

But as I came to the door of my home, drawing wearily nigh,
I heard with a boding heart a feeble whickering cry
Like a motherless yeanling's bleat ; and I stood in the dawn's grey light.
Afraid of I knew not what, sore spent with the toil of the night.

Then setting a quaking hand to the latch, I opened the door,
And shaking the cold from my heart, I stumbled across the floor
To the bed where she lay so quiet, calm-bosomed, in dreamless rest,
And the wailing baby clutched in vain at the lifeless breast.

I looked on the still white face, then sank with a cry by the bed,
And knew that the hand of death had stricken my whole joy dead –
My flock, my world, and my heart – with my love at a single blow ;
And I cried "I, too, will die !" and it seemed that life ebbed low

And the shadow of death drew nigh ; when I felt the touch on my cheek
Of a little warm hand out-thrust, and I heard that wail so weak ;
And knowing that not for me yet was there ease from love or strife,
I caught the babe to my breast and looked in the eyes of life.

IN THE ORCHARD

Sing no more songs of lovers dead
While jolly April weaves o'erhead
The boughs of blossom, white and red ;
Oh, look upon the living light
Caught in the nets of red and white,
That your sad dreams be put to flight !

Forget the shadow queens and kings
Who drank so deep of sorrow's springs ;
And tune to love the golden strings –
To love that laughs and leaps and sings
Through April hours on irised wings,
The happiest of all happy things.

To love – young love that never grieves
When summer's burden of bright leaves
About his head a shadow weaves ;
That dreads not autumn's waning gold,
Nor winds of winter, shrewd and cold,
Because he never groweth old.

We are no lovers, pale with dreams
Who languish by Lethean streams
Upon our bodies warm day gleams ;
And love that tingles warm and red
From sole of foot to crown of head
Is lord of all pale lovers dead !

THE MUSHROOM-GATHERERS

We rose an hour before the blink of day,
And with brown osier-baskets took our way
O'er pasture-land and paddock, glinting grey
With twilit dews that plashed about our feet.

Before me through the fleecy mist she went,
And, ever and anon, her body bent
To gather milk-white mushrooms, dew-besprent,
That huddled closely, waiting the noon heat.

She plucked the brittle domes with fingers deft,
And tenderly the nestling buttons reft
From their green, cosy beds, as right and left
She strayed to glean the meadow's snowy spoil.

By drowsy sheep and dewy-breathing beast
She moved ; nor from her aching labour ceased
Till dawn's pale glory shivered up the east ;
When, laden with the harvest of her toil –

Her brown hands resting lightly on her hips –
She stood a moment where the meadow dips,
Breathing the dawn with silent, parted lips
That with their dewy drinking glowed more red.

As o'er the bleak wold's edge, the young sun leapt,
And waked a world that happed in vapour slept,
Into the day with eager foot she stepped,
Her basket poised upon her lifted head.

And homeward with her heart my heart kept pace,
And nevermore, in any time or place,
Since I have seen the dawn light on her face,
Her heart shall lack my heart's companioning.

For us, while, bright against the dusky wood,
With morn-flushed brow and kindling hair she stood,
God made the day and saw that it was good ;
And love first taught the labouring heart to sing.

RED FOX

I hated him . . . His beard was red . . .
Red fox, red thief ! . . . Ah, God, that she –
She with the proud and lifted head
That never stooped to glance at me –
So fair and fancy-free, should wed
A slinking dog-fox such as he !

Was it last night I hated him ?
Last night ? It seems an age ago . . .
At whiles, my mind comes over dim
As if God's breath . . . yet, ever slow
And dull, too dull she . . . limb from limb
Last night I could have torn him, so !

My lonely bed was fire and ice
I could not sleep. I could not lie
I shut my hot eyes once or twice . . .
And saw a red fox slinking by . . .
A red dog-fox that turned back thrice
To mock me with a merry eye.

And so I rose to pace the floor . . .
And ere I knew, my clothes were on . . .
And as I stood outside the door,
Cold in the Summer moonlight shone
The gleaming barrel . . . and no more
I feared the fox, for fear was gone.

"The best of friends," I said, "must part . . ."
"The best of friends must part," I said :
And like the creaking of a cart
The words went wheeling through my head
"The best of friends . . . " and, in my heart,
Red fox, already lying dead !

I took the trackway through the wood,
Red fox had sought a woodland den,
When she . . . when she . . . but, 'twas not good
To think too much on her just then . . .
The woman must beware, who stood
Between two stark and fearless men.

The pathway took a sudden turn . . .
And in a trice my steps were stayed.
Before me, in the moonlit fern,
A young dog-fox and vixen played
With their red cubs beside the burn ...
And I stood trembling and afraid.

They frolicked in the warm moonlight –
A scuffling heap of heads and heels . . .
A rascal rush . . . a playful bite . . .
A scuttling brush, and frightened squeals . . .
A flash of teeth . . . a show of fight . . .
Then lively as a bunch of eels

Once more they gambolled in the brake,
And tumbled headlong in the stream,
Then scrambled gasping out to shake
Their sleek, wet, furry coats agleam.
I watched them, fearful and awake . . .
I watched them, hateless and adream.

The dog-fox gave a bark, and then
All ran to him : and, full of pride,
He took the trackway up the glen,
His family trotting by his side :
The young cubs nosing for the den,
With trailing brushes, sleepy-eyed.

And then it seems I must have slept –
Dropt dead asleep . . . dropt dead outworn.
I wakened, as the first gleam crept
Among the fern, and it was morn . . .
God's eye about their home had kept
Good watch, the night her son was born.

IN THE MEADOW

The smell of wet hay in the heat
All morning steaming round him rose,
As, in a kind of nodding doze,
Perched on the hard and jolting seat,
He drove the rattling, jangling rake
Round and around the Five Oaks Mead.
With that old mare he scarcely need
To drive at all, or keep awake.
Gazing with half-shut, sleepy eyes
At her white flanks and grizzled tail
That flicked and flicked, without avail,
To drive away the cloud of flies
That hovered, closing and unclosing,
A shimmering hum and humming shimmer,
Dwindling dim and ever dimmer
In his dazzled sight, till, dozing,
He seemed to hear a murmuring stream
And gaze into a rippling pool
Beneath thick branches dark and cool –
And gazing, gazing till a gleam
Within the darkness caught his eyes,
He saw there smiling up at him
A young girl's face, now rippling dim,
Now flashing clear . . .
                         Without surprise
He marked the eyes translucent blue,
The full red lips, that seemed to speak,
The curves of rounded chin and cheek,
The low, broad brow, sun-tanned . . .
                              He knew
That face, yet could not call to mind

Where he had seen it, and in vain
Strove to recall . . . when sudden rain
Crashed down and made the clear pool blind,
And it was lost . . .
                          And, with a jerk
That well-nigh shook him from his seat,
He wakened to the steamy heat
And clank and rattle.
                          Still at work
The stolid mare kept on ; and still
Over her hot white flanks the flies
Hung humming ; and his dazzled eyes
Closed gradually again, until
He dozed . . .
                          And stood within the door
Of Dinchill dairy, drinking there
Thirst-quenching draughts of stone-cold air –
The scoured white shelves and sanded floor
And shallow milk-pans creamy-white
Gleamed coldly in the dusky light . . .
And then he saw her, stooping down
Over a milk-pan, while her eyes
Looked up at him without surprise
Over the shoulder of her gown –
Her fresh print gown of speedwell blue . . .
The eyes that looked out of the cool
Untroubled crystal of the pool
Looked into his again.
                          He knew
Those eyes now . . .
                          From his dreamy doze
A sudden jolting of the rake
Aroused him.
                          Startled broad awake
He sat upright, lost in amaze
That he should dream of her – that lass !
And see her face within the pool !
He'd known her always. Why, at school
They'd sat together in the class.
He'd always liked her well enough,
Young Polly Dale – and they had played

76

At Prisoners' Base and Who's Afraid,
At Tiggy and at Blind Man's Buff,
A hundred times together . . .
                              Ay,
He'd always known her . . . It was strange,
Though he had noticed that a change
Had come upon her – she was shy,
And quieter, since she left school
And put her hair up – he'd not seen
Her face till from the glancing sheen
It looked up at him from the pool . . .
He'd always known her – every day
He'd nod to her as they would pass.
He'd always known her, as a lass . . .
He'd never know her just that way
Again now . . .
                    In a different wise
They'd meet – for how could he forget
His dream . . . The next time that they met
He'd look into a woman's eyes.

THE PLOUGH

He sniffed the clean and eager smell
Of crushed wild garlic, as he thrust
Beneath the sallows ; and a spell
He stood there munching a thick crust –
The fresh tang giving keener zest
To bread and cheese – and watched a pair
Of wagtails preening wing and breast,
Then running – flirting tails in air,
And pied plumes sleeked to silky sheen –
Chasing each other in and out
The wet wild garlic's white and green.

And then remembering, with a shout,
And rattle whirring, he ran back
Again into the Fair Maid's Mead,
To scare the rascal thieves and black
That flocked from far and near to feed

77

Upon the sprouting grain. As one
They rose with clapping, rustling wings –
Rooks, starlings, pigeons, in the sun
Circling about him in wide rings,
And plovers hovering over him
In mazy, interweaving flight –
Until it made his young wits swim
To see them up against the light,
A dazzling dance of black and white
Against the clear blue April sky –
Wings on wings in flashing flight
Swooping low and soaring high -
Swooping, soaring, fluttering, flapping,
Tossing, tumbling, swerving, dipping,
Chattering, cawing, creaking, clapping,
Till he felt his senses slipping,
And gripped his corncrake rattle tight,
And flourished it above his head
Till every bird was out of sight ;
And laughed, when all had flown and fled,
To think that he, and all alone,
Could put so many thieves to rout.

Then sitting down upon a stone
He wondered if the school were out –
The school where, only yesterday,
He's sat at work among his mates –
At work that now seemed children's play,
With pens and pencils, books and slates ;
Although he'd liked it well enough,
The hum and scuffling of the school,
And hadn't cared when Grim-and-Gruff
Would call him dunderhead and fool.

And he could see them sitting there,
His class-mates, in the lime-washed room,
With fingers inked and towzled hair –
Bill Baxter with red cheeks abloom,
And bright black eyes ; and Ginger Jim
With freckled face and solemn look,
Who'd wink a pale blue eye at him,
Then sit intent upon his book,

78

While, caught-a-giggle, he was caned.
He'd liked that room, he'd liked it all –
The window steaming when it rained ;
The sunlit dancing on the wall
Among the glossy charts and maps ;
The blotchy stain beside the clock
That only he of all the chaps
Knew for a chart of Dead Man's Rock
That lies in Tiger Island Bay –
The reef on which the schooners split
And founder, that would bear away
The treasure-chest of Cut-Throat-Kit,
That's buried under Black Bill's bones
Beneath the purple pepper-tree . . .
A trail of clean-sucked cherry-stones,
Which you must follow carefully,
Across the dunes of yellow sand
Leads winding upward from the beach
Till, with a pistol in each hand,
And cutlass 'twixt your teeth, you reach . . .

Plumping their far crops peacefully
Were plovers, pigeons, starlings, rooks,
Feeding on every side while he
Was in the land of storybooks.
He raised his rattle with a shout
And scattered them with yell and crake . . .
A man must mind what he's about
And keep his silly wits awake,
Not go wool-gathering, if he'd earn
His wage. And soon, no schoolboy now,
He'd take on a man's job, and learn
To build a rick, and drive the plough,
Like father . . .
     Up against the sky,
Beyond the spinney and the stream,
With easy stride and steady eye
He saw his father drive his team,
Turning the red marl gleaming wet
Into long furrows clean and true.
And dreaming there, he longed to set
His young hand to the ploughshare too.

BLOOM

Laburnum, lilac, honeysuckle, broom,
Syringa, rowan, hawthorn, guelder-rose,
Azalea, rose, and elder – summer glows
About me in sultry smother of scent and bloom
Shut in between the old walls' mossy brick :
Yet, as in the green and golden gloom I dream
In the drowsy dazzle of perfume and colour astream,
An upland odour stings me to the quick –
The shrewd remembered smell, sharp, clean and cold,
Of peat and moss, where never blossoms blow
Under the shadow of bleak whinstone scars
The summer-long, or only rarely show
Over black pools the sundew's stars of gold
Or grass-of-Parnassus' cold white scentless stars.

WORLDS

Through the pale forest of tall bracken-stalks
Whose interwoven fronds, a jade-green sky,
Above me glimmer infinitely high,
Towards my giant hand a beetle walks
In glistening emerald mail ; and as I lie
Watching his progress through huge grassy blades
And over pebble boulders, my own world fades
And shrinks to the vision of a beetle's eye.

Within that forest world of twilit green,
Ambushed with unknown perils, one endless day
I travel down the beetle-trail, between
Huge glossy boles, through green infinity . . .
Till flashes a glimpse of blue waves through the bracken
                                                    asway,
And my world is again a tumult of windy sea.

THE HAPPY FLIGHT

A multitude of starlings fly
Above me, flecking the blue sky
As far as the eye can see
With dark swift-shuttled patternings
Of whirring and exultant wings :
And all the crystal morning rings
With their wild whistling glee.

With sudden soft explosive sound
They rose as one bird from the ground
Where in the new-turned earth
They followed the loam-cleaving share,
Moved by one impulse to declare
Their life's delight and fill the air
With frenzy of shrill mirth.

And I, who plodded slowly by,
Brooding on war's long agony,
Felt my heart flutter, too,
With instant urge to scale the height
Of heaven with them in happy flight
And revel in the glittering light
Of winter's windy blue.

THE LONELY TREE

A twisted ash, a ragged fir,
A silver birch with leaves astir.

Men talk of forests broad and deep,
Where summer-long the shadows sleep.

Though I love forests deep and wide,
The lone tree on the bare hill-side,

The brave, wind-beaten, lonely tree,
Is rooted in the heart of me.

A twisted ash, a ragged fir,
A silver birch with leaves astir.

THE HAYMAKERS

Last night as in my bed awake
I fretted for the day
I heard the landrail's constant crake
Among the unmown hay ;

And in my head the thought that burned
And parched my lips and throat
Was like a wheel of fire that turned
On that hot aching note.

But with the crowing of the cock
The hours of waiting passed,
And slowly a shrill-chiming clock
Struck out the night at last.

I rose and soon my hot eyes roved
Over meadows dewy-deep,
That in the wind of morning moved
As if they turned from sleep ;

And where the crimson-rambler wreathed
The casement of my room
On my hot brow the cool air breathed
As on each fading bloom.

I watched the martin wheel and poise
Above his nested mate,
When clear through morning's murmurous noise
I heard a clicking gate

As down the dipping meadow-road
He bore with easy pace
His shouldered scythe, and brightly glowed
The dawnlight on his face.

All morn with swinging chorus blithe,
Unwearied through cool hours,
Was heard the swishing of the scythe
Among the grass and flowers ;

All morn behind the swaying row
Of shoulders brown and bare
I followed, glad at heart to know
He moved before me there ;

And as I laboured with the rake
Among the stricken grass,
Lightfooted in the mowers' wake
The happy hours did pass.

Too quick they went, and all too soon
The hour of resting came,
When over withering fields the noon
Hung like a still blue flame.

For as in shadow green and cool
He sank down wearily
Beside an alder-shaded pool,
He never turned to me ;

But looked upon the quivering blaze
With blue eyes cold and clear,
That never thrilled with love's amaze
Of joy and hope and fear.

And though afar beneath the briar
I watched him where he lay,
He knew not that my eyes afire
Burned brighter than the day.

And yet so loudly in my breast
Beat my tormented heart,
As if to rouse him from his rest,
I thought to see him start

As one awaked from midnight sleep
By knocking in the dark ;
But in his eyes' unclouded deep
There gleamed no kindling spark.

To-night no rails unresting crake
'Mid fallen grass and flowers ;
Naught stirs, and yet I lie awake
And count the crawling hours ;

And as I watch the glimmering light
I await dawn tremblingly,
Lest in the quiet of the night
His heart has turned to me –
Lest I should find the day had come,
As yet the day shall rise,
When he shall stand before me dumb
The fire within his eyes.

STARS

Who travelling through a midnight wood
Tilts up his chin to watch the stars
Will like enough trip over roots
Or back his shins against the knars :

But who, benighted in blind ways
Struggles to thrust close boughs apart
Will never win from out the wood
Unless the stars are in his heart.

THE WREN

She set the heavy washbasket down by the stile ;
And lay down, herself, in the shade, in a fragrant bed
Of wood-sanicle and sweet-woodruff, glad for a while
To be out of the steamy wash-house : when, over her head,
A wren piped out its shrill little roundelay :
And as she, through low green branches, looked at the blue day,
It seemed to her that she was a lassie again,
With a heart that sang in her bosom like that little wren.

THE SHEPHERD I

On a spur of golden fell, in the still September sunshine,
Above the flame of the bracken, a tall herd stands and whistles
Over the fleecy mist in the slack, to his faithful dogs
That scour the tawny shadowed slope of a further fell,
To fetch the straying flock to a fresher uncropped pasture.

He whistles, and waves an arm ; and the dogs on the far-off hillside
Respond to each note and each motion with quick and sure
                                                understanding,
Till the flurried ewes are gathered in a bleating bunch, and brought
Through the thinning mist of the slack to the crest of the sunlit fell,
Where the tall herd now stands silent, counting the dew-darkened
                                                fleeces.

Evermore in my heart will you stand thus, O shepherd,
On a spur of the golden fell in the still September sunshine,
Above the curling mist in the slack, and the bracken-flame,
Whistling your far-off dogs, or silently counting your flock,
Till the last long starless night shall fill my heart with slumber.

WILD BEES HAD BUILT. . . . .

Wild bees had built, while we had been from home,
A nest inside of the old-fashioned lock
Of the cottage door ; and choked it so with wax
The key wouldn't turn in the wards ; and we'd to climb
Into our home across the window-sill.
They must have started as soon as we'd turned our backs,
And set about their labour with right good will,
To have made themselves so secure in the nest, and block
The wards so badly in so short a time :
For they'd even started filling the honeycomb.

Yet, as we entered our little house once more,
It seemed to us not only the wild bees
Had been at work : for we found in each room a store
Of honeyed delight and golden memories.

85

WHISTLING WIND

Like unleashed lightening, Whistling Wind,
His snowy hound, flashed down the track,
Leaving the throng of grey and black
A dozen yards behind :

And, as she raced, it seemed his heart,
No longer prisoned in his breast,
A white streak leading all the rest –
Ay, even from the start,

Hot on the heels of the slick hare
That never glanced to left or right,
A dazzling wildfire of delight,
Flashed through the whistling air !

BROWN WATERS

Love, have you, too, been listening
To the singing of the burn,
The singing of brown waters
That thresh and froth and churn
Among the basalt boulders
Through brakes of withered fern ?

Love, have you, too, been listening
To that music clear and cold,
The song of snow-fed waters,
Than all man's songs more old,
And heard by the first shepherd
Who builded the first fold ?

Oh, let not that cold music
Of water upon stone
Steal you from the warm ingle,
To brood too long alone,
Till love dies to the music
Of water upon stone.

SONG IN RAIN

The heather was wet beneath us –
But we, what did we care !
Brown and wet was the heather
As your tangled wet brown hair :
While the larks in the rainy lift were singing ;
And our hearts were as larks in the air.

The larks soared into the rain-cloud
That could not quench their mirth –
The golden fire of their singing :
And we lay on the wet brown earth,
In the drench of rain and golden music
That ended drought and dearth.

HE IS TENDER WITH THE BEASTS . . .

He is tender with the beasts,
Just as tender as can be ;
But his eyes have never glanced
Once at me.

Little things like calves and lambs
Bring the lovelight to his eye ;
But he never seems to know
I am by.

Though the other lads all swear
I am handsomer than all,
I would give my soul to be
Weak and small.

THE HOMERS

He flung his pigeons up into the air ;
And watched them wheel, and then steer nor'-nor'-west,
Unfaltering on the homeward course : and now
A pang of longing shot through his proud breast

To soar into the blue on clapping wings,
And follow in as swift and sure a flight ;
And, with the birds, in one quick flashing hour
Reach home, instead of trudging half the night –

With them arrive, while still the evening sun
Kindled the cottage windows, and the eyes
Of wife and bairns, who watched, even now, to greet
Those travellers homing from far unknown skies.

THE MOWER

He limps as he walks, and his mind is awry ;
But he swings his scythe as sure and clean
As any mower beneath the sky :
His wits are dull, but his blade is keen.

My wits are keen : but a stumbling pen
Only expresses in halting rhyme
What he does over and over again
In easy rhythm and perfect time.

PRESAGE OF WINTER

White as hoarfrost, the dewy gossamers
Mantle the furze ;
And in the sparse turf glimmer snowy-white
And dewy mushrooms, sprung up in the night.

Chill is the morning air, as with the breath
Of winter o'er the heath ;
And, though the noon burn hot, at eve the chill
And heavy dews will drench the naked hill.

Fled are the summer days, although September,
As the last ember
Of dying fires, glows golden yet, and fled
Warm nights when we might seek a heather-bed.

White soon with mantling snows the fells will lie
Beneath the sky,
White under the pale winter sun ; and white
Beneath the steely-gleaming stars all night.

Gold was our summer under the gold sun ;
And, now its done,
Shall not our dreams, O Love, still burn with gold,
When snows are piled above us white and cold ?

CURLEW

That note – that note !
Comes there so clear a call from any throat,
So clear a call to me
Back to the hills, the hills of memory ?

The curlew's call
Is April sunshine on cold fells, and all
Rapture of youth to me,
Calling me to the hills, the hills of memory.

THE WINDY NIGHT

All night the wind lashed at the pane
And slashed the glass with squalls of rain –
Wave after wave of tempest crashed
Against the little house in vain.

All night the man tossed in his bed,
And lost and found and lost the thread
Of intertwining thoughts that crossed
In mazy tangles in his head.

If but the wind would cease, he knew
He should lay hold upon the clue
Of all he now misunderstood . . .
But still the tempest blew and blew !

NOVEMBER GOLD

With bended back and nose nigh touching toes,
Down the unending mangel-wurzel rows
All days he goes,
Lifting the roots, and slicing off the tops :
And, even to ease his back, he seldom stops,
Although the copse
That borders the Ten Acre is aflare
In the pale flame of blue November air
With gold more rare
And richly glowing than the dreams that hold
The hungry heart of man with wealth untold
Of fabled gold.

With bended back and nose nigh touching toes,
Down the unending mangel-wurzel rows
Heedless he goes,
Earning a scanty wage with his sharp knife
To feed the hungry brood he and his wife
Have brought to life :
Heedless he goes of birch and beech that hold
For a brief season only wealth untold

Of fabled gold,
That only hold their pride of gold until
That night wind, sweeping down from Wilbury Hill,
Their treasure spill.

SNOW IN MAY

A week before, the storm would scarce have mattered,
Or a week later, when the fruit had set ;
But at that moment it was sheer disaster –
The blizzard swooping down upon the valley
Of orchards, one vast rose of sunlit bloom
An hour ago. The tragical wild beauty
Of whirling flakes among the blossomed branches
Could not appease the anger in his heart
At all that promise wasted, all those months
Of labour brought to naught, but touched with terror
The spirit in him that must fight for life
Against such hazards, gods that with a gesture
Of idle malice could blast all his hopes.
Outwitting careful craft and foresight – he
In his little orchard-plot of fifteen acres
Pitted against the forces of the sky.
The merciless blind furies that unhindered
Range the illimitable airs of heaven.
A man against the incalculable weather –
Drought, Arctic wind and the black blighting East
And ruthless pests and scourges – one man against
The unaccountable capricious gods !
Yet there were years of plenty, as of dearth,
Fat years as well as lean, when the fates seemed
In indolent indifference, almost kind,
And played no havoc with the apple-harvest.
And, even at the worst, had he not snatched

Out of disaster something ? As the blizzard
In terrible beauty whirled through blossomed boughs,
His very anger kindled in his heart
A flame of life more fervent than a succession
Of easy harvests could bring into being.

The fighting flame of human fortitude
No malice or caprice of reckless gods
Has ever quenched since from the dust man rose
To take up the unequal desperate struggle –
The flame that quickens in adversity
And, blazing to fresh fury from defeat,
Victorious o'er the victor leaps to heaven !

The storm had passed ; and now the sun shone out,
Smiling upon the valley's devastation,
Boughs overburdened with the mocking bloom
Of shrouding snow, death to the living blossom
That one brief hour since under the same sun
Had glowed, one rosy promise of golden harvest.

THE SHEPHERD II

Within a wattled cote on the Ridgeway Down
Tending his labouring ewes by the faint light
Of his horn-lantern, through the cloudy night
The shepherd hears high overhead, a flight
Of raiders making for some Western town.

Shielding the light within his coat, he stands
For a brief idle moment harkening
To that deep drone of death upon the wing ;
Then turns to his own business, to bring
Innocent life to birth with tender hands.

BEAUTY FOR ASHES

You may burn the golden glory of the gorse,
But the roots into the rocky earth run deep,
And the living bush will only glow to rarer fire of beauty
When at last beneath the mould you lie asleep.

Beauty dies not though you blast and lay it waste,
Though you turn the whole earth to a cinder-heap,
From the ashes of your factories once again the ever-living
Shall awake one April morning out of sleep.

THE TWO WORLD WARS

BREAKFAST

We ate our breakfast lying on our backs,
Because the shells were screeching overhead.
I bet a rasher to a loaf of bread
That Hull United would beat Halifax
When Jimmy Stainthorp played full-back instead
Of Billy Bradford. Ginger raised his head
And cursed, and took the bet ; and dropt back dead.
We ate our breakfast lying on our backs,
Because the shells were screeching overhead.

HIT

Out of the sparking sea
I drew my tingling body clear, and lay
On a low ledge the livelong summer day,
Basking, and watching lazily
White sails in Falmouth Bay.

My body seemed to burn
Salt in the sun that drenched in through and through
Till every particle glowed clean and new
And slowing seemed to turn
To lucent amber in a world of blue . . .

I felt a sudden wrench –
A trickle of warm blood –
And found that I was sprawling in the mud
Among the dead men in the trench.

NIGHTMARE

They gave him a shilling,
They gave him a gun,
And so he's gone killing
The Germans, my son.

I dream of that shilling –
I dream of that gun –
And it's they that are killing
The boy who's my son.

RAINING

The night I left my father said :
"You'll go and do some stupid thing.
You've no more sense in that fat head
Than Silly Billy Witterling.

"Not sense to come in when it rains –
Not sense enough for that, you've got.
You'll get a bullet through your brains,
Before you know, as like as not."

And now I'm lying in the trench
And shells and bullets through the night
Are raining in a steady drench,
I'm thinking the old man was right.

HILL-BORN

I sometimes wonder if it's really true
I ever knew
Another life
Than this unending strife
With unseen enemies in lowland mud,
And wonder if my blood
Thrilled ever to the tune
Of clean winds blowing through an April noon
Mile after sunny mile
On the green ridges of the Windy Gile.

DESERT NIGHT

What do you see as you pace the night
To and fro
On sentry-go ?
The full moon trancing with light
Cheviot silvered with snow !

What do you smell as you pace the night
On sentry-beat
With burning feet ?
Redesdale in morning light
Foaming with meadowsweet !

What do you hear as you pace the night
Of breathless fear
With straining ear ?
The roar of the frothing white
Lasher of Otterburn Weir.

COMRADES

As I was marching in Flanders
A ghost kept step with me –
Kept step with me and chuckled
And muttered ceaselessly :

"Once I too marched in Flanders,
The very spit of you,
And just a hundred years since,
To fall at Waterloo.

"They buried me in Flanders
Upon the field of blood,
And long I've lain forgotten
Deep in the Flemish mud.

"But now you march in Flanders,
The very spit of me ;
To the ending of the day's march
I'll bear you company."

THE QUIET

I could not understand the sudden quiet –
The sudden darkness – in the crash of fight,
The din and glare of day quenched in a twinkling
In utter starless night.

I lay an age and idly gazed at nothing,
Half-puzzled that I could not lift my head ;
And then I knew somehow that I was lying
Among the other dead.

OTTERBURN

The lad who went to Flanders –
Otterburn, Otterburn –
The lad who went to Flanders,
And never will return –

Though low he lies in Flanders,
Beneath the Flemish mud,
He hears through all his dreaming
The Otterburn in flood.

And though there be in Flanders
No clear and singing streams,
The Otterburn runs singing
Of summer through his dreams.

And when peace comes to Flanders,
Because it comes too late,
He'll still lien there, and listen
To the Otterburn in spate –

The lad who went to Flanders –
Otterburn, Otterburn –
The lad who went to Flanders,
And never will return.

"O WHAT SAW YOU ?"

O what saw you in Flanders
Fighting for the king ?
Rain and mud, and rain and mud,
And never another thing.

O what saw you in Babylon
Fighting for the king ?
Sun and sand, and sun and sand,
And never another thing.

Are there no burns in Flanders,
No tumbling burns that sing :
Are there no braes in Babylon
Bonnie with broom and ling

There are no burns in Flanders,
No tumbling burns that sing :
There are no braes in Babylon
Bonnie with broom and ling.

Then I'll not go to Flanders
Nor yet to Babylon,
But keep to my own country's
Clean rain and kindly sun.

Who will may dream of Baghdad
And sigh for Samarkand –
I'll live content with the windy bent
Of green Northumberland.

THE LUCK

If I'd not got him, he'd have got me :
If I'd not shot him, he'd have shot me . . .

Over and over in my head
Each night before I go to bed –
Half-dozing in the cosy glow,
And thinking of twelve years ago –
The rhyme keeps turning and re-turning.

In No-Man's-Land we met – a flare
Went up, and showed him crouching there –
The luck was mine ; so in my chair
I sit and watch the beech-logs burning,
I sit beside the hearth ; but he
In No-Mans'-Land is 'waiting me ;
And every night his bony hand
Beckons me back to No-Man's-Land.

And by my side my mother knits,
Happy to have me still ; she sits
And knits and knits contentedly :
And somewhere too, in Germany
Another mother sits - but she,
What does she think as she knits ?

If I'd not got him, he'd have got me :
If I'd not shot him, he'd have shot me.

REVEILLE

Still bathed in its moonlight slumber the little white house by the cedar
Stands silent against the red dawn ;
And nothing I know of who sleeps there, to the travail of day yet
                                                    unwakened,
Behind the blue curtains undrawn ;

But I dream as we march down the roadway, ringing
Loud and rime-white in the moonlight,
Of a little dark house on a hill
Wherein when the battle is over, to rapture of day yet unwakened,
We shall slumber as dreamless and still.

AFTERMATH

Till, as I crossed the Strand, it flashed on me
That he'd not been in khaki, when few men
Were out of uniform, though I knew he
Had fought at Passchendaele ; but, even then

I failed to gather the significance
Of our encounter in the street, till I
Chanced on the news that he'd been killed in France
The very afternoon he passed me by –

He passed me by, as one who walks in dream,
Without a smile or word, to my surprise :
And then I knew the meaning of the gleam
In those strange still unrecognising eyes.

99

NOVEMBER 11TH

She wakened in the night to hear
Her son's voice moaning in her ear –
I cannot rest, I cannot sleep . . .
Day after day I hear you weep,
And even in deepest slumber, yet
Your heart remembers. Oh, forget,
Forget your son, dear mother ! I,
Till you forget me, cannot die,
I cannot wholly die, for still
About the battle-shattered hill
My ghost must wander restlessly
While anyone remembers me . . .
Long since the living folk I knew
Have all forgotten, all but you ;
And sore I long to rest, to die
Once and for ever, long to lie
At peace, and sleep and sleep . . . but I,
I cannot sleep till you forget.

THE LOOK-OUT

As, lightless, up the Skaagerack they stole,
Alert for danger from the sky or sea,
And eerily an unknown sea-fowl wailed,
The look-out saw strangely familiar forms
Arising from the waters quietly
And gathering round the trawler in the dim
And moony haze ; and knew within his soul
Old shipmates, lost in action, who had sailed
These seas with him and braved their blasting storms,
Had roused from restless sleep to welcome him.

BACCHANAL

Into the twilight of Trafalgar Square
They pour from every quarter, banging drums
And tootling penny trumpets – to a blare
Of tin mouth-organs, while a sailor strums
A solitary banjo, lads and girls
Locked in embraces in a wild dishevel
Of flags and streaming hair, with curdling skirls
Surge in a frenzied reeling panic revel.

Lads who so long have stared death in the face,
Girls who so long have tended death's machines.
Released from the long terror shriek and prance –
And, watching them, I see the outrageous dance,
The frantic torches and the tambourines
Tumultuous on the midnight hills of Thrace.

(November 1918)

THE ABBEY TOWER

As, wounded, on the Libyan sand he lies,
The broad embattled tower
Familiar to his eyes
From childhood's earliest hour,
Dispelling the cold gloom
Above him seems to rise
Kindled by sunset, all about it flying
Jackdaws with gilded wing and burnished plume :
And in his eyes as he is dying
Their homely cawing and the old careless chimes
Recall the innocent days
Of war-unshadowed times ;
And once again with other boys he plays
Happily on the green slopes of the Sele
In the late sunset-light
While from the Abbey tower resounds the peal
Of ringers practising on Thursday night.

THE FATIGUE

Someone else went in my place. As it happened, that morning a corporal,
Knowing no more than myself I was detailed for draft, had despatched me
On fatigue with a convoy of lorries to Woolwich to bring back manure for
The gardens of villas whose lawns had been ploughed up for planting potatoes :
And bored to the bone by just loafing about, or by sweeping out billets –
Six men fooling round at a job that a housemaid could do before breakfast –
Or by picking up cigarette-ends and spent matches, or out of the ash-pit
Collecting the cinders again (for coal had run short, and the fires of
The lords in the offices still must be kept blazing half up the chimney),
I was glad to be moving at last, to be going somewhere, to be riding
In the icy bright light, as the lumbering lorry crunched over the crisp snow,
Drinking the sun-golden wine of the morning that went to our heads and
Set us all stamping and shouting and singing in rollicking chorus
As we jolted and swung on the lurching lorry across the white country . . .

So, when the roll came to be called of the oversea draft, there was no one
To answer for Private Gibson, M.T. 381907 ;
And some other man had to pack up his kit in a deuce of a hurry
To fill up the gap in the ranks and set out for France in my place,
While I rode singing to Woolwich, rode on, knowing nothing about it.

And when at length we reached Woolwich, we leapt from the lorries to tackle
The snow-buried mounds of manure, and thrust in our forks with a flourish
Through the cold and crystalline crust, discovering the rich steaming treasure
Of gold dung, and easily heaved it, heaping it high in the lorries,
Delighting at last to be doing a man's job again, to be sweating
At something worth while, at something to feed the old earth and to nourish
Fresh life when so much else was dying, and men thought of little
                                        but slaughter . . .

Then back with the golden-heaped lorries we rode once again to the billets,
Happy and hungry – and I, knowing nothing as yet of my 'crime' –
'Absent from draft' – I came back . . .
                              But he who had gone in my place,
He who had gone oversea in my stead, who was taking my chances,
Playing my hazards with death, I know not if he ever returned.

BACK

They ask me where I've been,
And what I've done and seen.
But what can I reply
Who know it wasn't I,
But someone just like me,
Who went across the sea
And with my head and hands
Killed men in foreign lands . . .
Though I must bear the blame
Because he bore my name.

LAMENT

We who are left, how shall we look again
Happily in the sun, or feel the rain,
Without remembering how they who went
Ungrudgingly, and spent
Their all for us, loved, too, the sun and rain ?

A bird among the rain-wet lilac sings –
But we, how shall we turn to little things
And listen to the birds and winds and streams
Made holy by their dreams,
Nor feel the heart-break in the heart of things ?

FRIENDS AND POETS

TREES

For Lascelles Abercrombie

The flames half-lit the cavernous mystery
Of the wide-branching elm that loomed profound
 In Summer leafage, towering from the ground
To midnight stars in tranced serenity,
As, under the quiet of that ageless tree,
In a rapt dreaming ring we lay around
The flickering faggots, once again spellbound
By old words moving in new harmony.

And, as you read, arose before our eyes
A rarer tree of visionary birth
To brave the weather of eternal skies,
Crested with stars, yet, rooted deep in earth,
Its legend-haunted branches laced with gleams
Of friendly firelight and the light of dreams.

RUPERT BROOKE

I

Your face was lifted to the golden sky
Ablaze beyond the black roofs of the square
As flame on flame leapt, flourishing in air
Its tumult of red stars exultantly
To the cold constellations dim and high ;
And, as we neared, the roaring ruddy flare
Kindled to gold your throat and brow and hair
Until you burned, a flame of ecstasy.

The golden head goes down into the night
Quenched in cold gloom – and yet again you stand
Beside me now with lifted face alight
As, flame to flame and fire to fire, you burn . . .
Then, recollecting, laughingly you turn
And look into my eyes and take my hand.

II

Once in my garret – you being far away
Tramping the hills and breathing upland air,
Or so I fancied – brooding in my chair,
I watched the London sunlight feeble and grey
Dapple my desk, too tired to labour more,
When, looking up, I saw you standing there,
Although I'd caught no footstep on the stair,
Like sudden April at my open door.

Though now beyond earth's farthest hills you fare,
Song-crowned, immortal, sometimes it seems to me
That if I listen very quietly
Perhaps I'll hear your footstep on the stair
And see you, standing with your angel air,
Fresh from the uplands of eternity.

III

Your eyes rejoiced in colour's ecstasy,
Fulfilling even their uttermost desire,
When, over a great sunlit field afire
With windy poppies streaming like a sea
Of scarlet flame that flaunted riotously
Among green orchards of that western shire,
You gazed as though your heart could never tire
Of life's red flood in summer revelry.

And as I watched you, little thought had I
How soon beneath the dim, low-drifting sky
Your soul should wander down the darkling way
With eyes that peer a little wistfully,
Half-glad, half-sad, remembering, as they see
Lethean poppies shrivelling ashen grey.

October chestnuts showered their perishing gold
Over us as beside the stream we lay
In the Old Vicarage garden that blue day,
Talking of verse and all the manifold
Delights a little net of words may hold,
While in the sunlight water-voles at play
Dived under a trailing crimson bramble spray,
And walnuts thudded ripe on soft black mould.

Your soul goes down unto a darker stream
Alone, O friend, yet even in death's deep night
Your eyes may grow accustomed to the dark,
And Styx for you may have the ripple and gleam
Of your familiar river, and Charon's bark
Tarry by that old garden of your delight.

TO THE MEMORY OF RUPERT BROOKE

He's gone,
I do not understand :
I only know
That as he turned to go
And waved his hand
In his young eyes a sudden glory shone,
And I was dazzled by a sunset glow,
And he was gone.

23rd April 1915

GRAY'S INN

To Edward Marsh

The bell rings, the key clicks, the door swings open,
And the lodge-porter scans my face. *Good-night !* –
Good-night, sir ! The door clashes ; and he turns
Again to his evening paper in his box,
Keen to resume the interrupted murder ;
And little dreams that he let in with me
Two others, spirits whose immortal brows
No mortal eye may scan.

On such a night
In nineteen-twelve, when yet the world went well,
Three living friends, thrilled to the core with London –
The riot, the glitter, the peril, out of the glare
And clatter of Holborn, into shadowed courts
And customary calm we passed by dark
Deserted offices, until we came
To the great iron gate of the old garden,
Wherein a quiet company of trees
Live their untroubled lives at London's heart.

And, as we halted, hushed in their still presence,
As pilgrims coming to a secret grove,
Shadowed and heavy-foliaged, they lifted
Unquivering branches to the summer stars
That sprinkled the blue night with vagrant silver –
In universal wandering unaware
As those earth-rooted and sequestered trees
Of the smoke and smoulder of man's fevered life,
That, but too soon, burst into such a blaze
As burned up half the world, and in its fury
Consumed the generations of young men ;
And, with them, Denis Browne and Rupert Brooke –
Denis, with all his music in his heart,
And Rupert, with his first songs on his lips.

In foreign fields they lie to-night – but still
The trees serenely lift their stirless branches
To the indifferent stars. Yet, no sad shades

Are they who stand beside me, but young spirits,
Song-aureoled, with laughter in their eyes ;
While I, an ageing man between them, seem
A furtive purposeless ghost, haunting the shadow
Of ghostly trees beneath cold ghostly stars.

1925

TO JOHN DRINKWATER

You speak to-night
Of Dymock and its daffodils ;
And the great audience listens with delight :
And yet, and yet,
They cannot know the ecstasy that fills
My heart to hear you – they, to whom the words
Bring only pleasure tinged with no regret.

Dymock and daffodils and days of song
Before the war had scattered us apart . . .
And still in Dymock fields the daffodils
Dance to the singing of the birds ;
And once again my heart,
Awakened by your words,
Dances with them a moment – as it danced
In days of old
Entranced
In singing dreams of dancing gold,
In days of old before the world went wrong.

RUSSELL HILLARD LOINES

You'll come again and see us soon ? I called,
As he released the clutch ; and, with a smile,
He turned. *We'll do our darnedest !* he sang out :
And then the car sped down the bough-hung road
Through Little Malvern, where, in its green nook.
Under the naked scarp of Hereford Beacon,
The embowered Priory Church enshrines old dreams
And holy memories.

                      This was our farewell.
He came no more – only the message came,
The unbelievable word that he was dead,
That eager ardent life unquenchable,
Or so it had seemed to us, burnt out so soon !
And now my heart enshrines dear memories –
The letter from America from Brooke,
Whose golden flame had even briefer life,
Telling of these new friends who, even then,
Were on their way to visit us : the day,
A winter day in the old incredible time
Before the war, a silver-frosted day,
When Russell and Katherine walked from Ledbury
To see us in our cottage at the cross-roads . . .

Then three years later, when so much had happened –
The world collapsed ; and Rupert, dead at Skyros,
A second meeting in America . . .
The ferry on the way to Staten Island,
Leaving behind the huge black thrusting wedges,
Spangled with multitudinous white lights,
That cut into the cold blue night from which
The wintry stars drooped crystal lustres over
New York's defiant Babel-builded towers :
Then many walks and talks on that fair island,
Which seemed just like a little bit of England
That, somehow breaking loose, had braved the sheer
Extravagant perils of Atlantic waters,
And come to anchor on the other side –
Such walks and talks along the snowy roads,

Or by the hearth of blazing birchen logs ;
Or, when the summer came, on starry nights
In that still garden, lit by moon-white roses,
Yet dimly glowing, and the flickering twinkle
As, one by one, about us fireflies flashed,
Until the lucent dusk was all a dazzle
Of glancing dithering lightnings, as we sat,
Now talking, and now communing in silence ;
And gazing over the Narrows, from our retreat
Of rose-hung, faery-lanthorned peace, to where
The riotous night of Coney Island flared
Like the red fury of some alien star . . .

Then three years later still, when war was over,
And youth had perished in us with the young
Who died for us through those relentless years,
That each had seemed an aeon of agony –
Again in England, one long golden day
High on the western slope of Worcester Beacon,
Looking across green rolling Herefordshire
To the blue rampart of the hills of Wales ;
And musing on a marble hill in Skyros
That held the dust of him who made us friends . . .

So little now they seem, set down in words,
These memories – yet so much ! though only they
Who knew him can recall how much – for hills
And towers and lights and roses and sea-washed islands,
The Atlantic, England and America,
Poetry and philosophy laced with laughter,
Are symbols of his spirit ; and may not still
Its sheer unquenchable light burn through my words
Till they rekindle in the hearts of men
The fervour of that heart of lambent flame ?

1925

110

THE GOLDEN ROOM

To Geraldine

Do you remember that still summer evening
When, in the cosy cream-washed living-room
Of The Old Nailshop, we all talked and laughed –
Our neighbours from The Gallows, Catherine
And Lascelles Abercrombie ; Rupert Brooke ;
Elinor and Robert Frost, living a while
At Little Iddens, who'd brought over with them
Helen and Edward Thomas ? In the lamplight
We talked and laughed ; but, for the most part, listened
While Robert Frost kept on and on and on,
In his slow New England fashion, for our delight,
Holding us with shrewd turns and racy quips,
And the rare twinkle of his grave blue eyes ?

We sat there in the lamplight, while the day
Died from rose-latticed casements, and the plovers
Called over the low meadows, till the owls
Answered them from the elms, we sat and talked –

Now, a quick flash from Abercrombie ; now,
A murmured dry half-heard aside from Thomas ;
Now, a clear laughing word from Brooke, and then
Again Frost's rich and ripe philosophy,
That had the body and tang of good draught-cider,
And poured as clear a stream.

'Twas in July
Of nineteen-fourteen that we sat and talked :
Then August brought the war, and scattered us.
Now, on the crest of an Aegean isle,
Brooke sleeps, and dreams of England : Thomas lies
'Neath Vimy Ridge, where he, among his fellows,
Died, just as life had touched his lips to song.

And nigh as ruthlessly has life divided
Us who survive ; for Abercrombie toils
In a black Northern town, beneath the glower
Of hanging smoke ; and in America
Frost farms once more ; and, far from the Old Nailshop
We sojourn by the Western sea.

And yet,
Was it for nothing that the little room,
All golden in the lamplight, thrilled with golden
Laughter from hearts of friends that summer night ?
Darkness has fallen on it ; and the shadow
May never more be lifted from our hearts
That went through those black years of war, and I live.

And still, whenever men and women gather
For talk and laughter on a summer night,
Shall not the lamp rekindle ; and the room
Glow once again alive with light and laughter ;
And, like a singing star in time's abyss,
Burn golden-hearted through oblivion ?

TO EDWARD MARSH

The night we saw the stacks of timber blaze
To terrible golden fury, young and strong
He watched between us with dream-dazzled gaze
Aflame and burning like a god of song,
As we together stood against the throng
Drawn from the midnight of the city ways.

To-night the world about us is ablaze
And he is dead, is dead . . . Yet, young and strong,
He watches us still with deathless gaze
Aflame and burning like a god of song,
As we together stand against the throng
Drawn from the bottomless midnight of hell's ways.

In memory of Rupert Brooke 10th June 1915

THE THREE POETS

To-day, in glancing through the Sunday paper,
I chanced upon the news, Sturge Moore had died –
Sturge Moore, the last of the three friends, whom I,
A country lad on holiday, first met
When Binyon strolled with him and Yeats together
Into a Holborn teashop, and beckoned me
To come and join them at their table – Binyon,
Grave-eyed and gentle ; Yeats, with lank dark hair
And dark eyes flashing like the moonlit waters
Of some lone Irish lough ; and Sturge Moore, faun-like,
With a long straggly beard of russet brown :
And I remember how I sat enthralled,
A raw lad listening to those poets talking –
Those poets in their thirties and the prime
Of their creative energy, discussing
Tolstoy's heretical 'What is Art ?' – Yeats, pouring
A stream of scintillating eloquence
In his broad-vowelled brogue ; and Sturge Moore, piping
Keen commentary ; while, for the most part, Binyon
Sat silent, pondering like some Indian god
Rapt in calm introspective meditation.

And, now an old man, I recall how I
Last saw those poets – Sturge Moore, with snowy beard
And dreamy eyes declaiming a new work
To a hushed circle in his house at Hampstead –
A visionary mosaic of coloured words
That, with a craft, half-poet's and half-painter's,
Aural and visual, to the inner eye
Revealed in rhythm the old heroic world ;

Yeats, with his shock of grey hair, slowly pacing
The platform, waiting for the Irish Mail
At Euston, his old dark eyes still aflame
With the unquenchable genius that burned
Fed with an ever fuller sense of life
Ever to fierier intensity
As he grew old ; then Binyon on that day
In the third year of the world-war's renewal
When Summer rain drenched round his downland home

And we together sat by the log-fire,
And I, remembering that earlier time
In days of peace when first I heard him read
In his snug book-lined room in Cowley Street
While over night-hushed Westminster the stars
Kept watch above a yet unshattered world,
Now listened once again with blood that pulsed
Responsive to the rhythm and the rapture
As he to me with undiminished vigour
Read his last poems in the resonant voice
Whose organ-tones still echo in my heart.

And, in these dire and dreadful days, as I
Muse on these memories, I long once more to be
That stripling sitting in a Holborn teashop
With heart that kindles to the eloquence
Of those three poets who have left so rich
A heritage, still in the prime of life
Discoursing on the theme that was the breath
And being of their earthly pilgrimage.

1944

AT SEA

DEVIL'S EDGE

All night I lay on Devil's Edge,
Along an overhanging ledge
Between the sky and sea :
And as I rested 'waiting sleep,
The windless sky and soundless deep
In one dim, blue infinity
Of starry peace encompassed me.

And I remembered, drowsily,
How 'mid the hills last night I'd lain
Beside a singing moorland burn ;
And waked at dawn, to feel the rain
Fall on my face, as on the fern
That drooped about my heather-bed :
And how by noon the wind had blown
That last grey shred from out the sky,
And blew my homespun jacket dry,
As I stood on the topmost stone
That crowns the cairn on Hawkshaw Head,
And caught a gleam of far-off sea ;
And heard the wind sing in the bent
Like those far waters calling me :
When, my heart answering to the call,
I followed down the seaward stream,
By silent pool and singing fall :
Till with a quiet, keen content,
I watched the sun, a crimson ball,
Shoot through grey seas a fiery gleam,
Then sink in opal deeps from sight.

And with the coming on of night,
The wind had dropped : and as I lay,
Retracing all the happy day,
And gazing long and dreamily
Across the dim, unsounding sea,
Over the far horizon came
A sudden sail of amber flame ;

And soon the new moon rode on high
Through cloudless deeps of crystal sky.

Too holy seemed the night for sleep :
And yet I must have slept, it seems ;
For, suddenly, I woke to hear
A strange voice singing, shrill and clear,
Down in a gully black and deep
That cleft the beetling crag in twain.
It seemed the very voice of dreams
That drive hag-ridden souls in fear
Through echoing, unearthly vales,
To plunge in black, slow-crawling streams,
Seeking to drown that cry, in vain . . .
Or some sea creature's voice that wails
Through blind, white banks of fog unlifting
To God-forgotten sailors drifting
Rudderless to death . . .
As as I heard,
Though no wind stirred,
An icy breath
Was in my hair . . .
And clutched my heart with cold despair.
But, as the wild song died away,
There came a faltering break
That shivered to a sobbing fall ;
And seemed half-human, after all . . .

And yet, what foot could find a track
In that deep gully, sheer and black . . .
And singing wildly in the night !
So, wondering, I lay awake,
Until the coming of the light
Brought day's familiar presence back.

Down by the harbour-mouth that day,
A fisher told the tale to me.
Three months before, while out at sea,
Young Philip Burn was lost, though how,
None knew, and none would ever know.
The boat becalmed at noonday lay . . .
And not a ripple on the sea . . .

And Philip standing in the bow,
When his six comrades went below
To sleep away an hour or so,
Dog-tired with working day and night,
While he kept watch . . . and not a sound
They heard, until at set of sun
They woke ; and coming up, they found
The deck was empty, Philip gone . . .
Yet not another boat in sight . . .
And not a ripple on the sea.
How he had vanished, none could tell,
They only knew the lad was dead
They'd left but now, alive and well . . .
And he, poor fellow, newly-wed . . .
And when they broke the news to her,
She spoke no word to anyone :
But sat all day, and would not stir –
Just staring, staring in the fire,
With eyes that never seemed to tire ;
Until, at last, the day was done,
And darkness came ; when she would rise,
And seek the door with queer, wild eyes ;
And wander singing all the night
Unearthly songs beside the sea :
But always the first blink of light
Would find her back at her own door.

'Twas winter when I came once more
To that old village by the shore :
And as, at night, I climbed the street,
I heard a singing, low and sweet,
Within a cottage near at hand ;
And I was glad awhile to stand
And listen by the glowing pane :
And as I hearkened, that sweet strain
Brought back the night when I had lain
Awake on Devil's Edge . . .

And now I knew the voice again,
So different, free of pain and fear –
Its terror turned to tenderness –

And yet the same voice none the less,
Though singing now so true and clear :
And drawing nigh the window-ledge,
I watched the mother sing to rest
The baby snuggling to her breast.

SOLWAY FORD

He greets you with a smile from friendly eyes,
But never speaks nor rises from his bed :
Beneath the green night of the sea he lies,
The whole world's waters weighing on his head.

The empty wain made slowly over the sand,
And he with hands in pockets by the side
Was trudging, deep in dream, the while he scanned
With blue unseeing eyes the far-off tide,
When, stumbling in a hole, with startled neigh
His young horse reared and, snatching at the rein,
He slipped :   the wheels crushed on him as he lay ;
Then, tilting over him, the lumbering wain
Turned turtle, as the plunging beast broke free
And made for home ; and, pinioned and half-dead,
He lay and listened to the far-off sea
And seemed to hear it surging overhead
Already, though 'twas full an hour or more
Until high-tide when Solway's shining flood
Should sweep the shallow firth from shore to shore.
He felt a salty tingle in his blood
And seemed to stifle, drowning :   then again
He knew that he must lie a lingering while
Before the sea might close upon his pain,
Although the advancing waves had scarce a mile
To travel, creeping nearer inch by inch
With little runs and sallies over the sand.
Cooped in the dark, he felt his body flinch
From each cold wave as it drew nearer hand.
He saw the froth of each oncoming crest
And felt the tugging of the ebb and flow
And waves already breaking over his breast –

Though still far-off they murmured faint and low,
Yet creeping nearer inch by inch, and now
He felt the cold drench of the drowning wave
And the salt cold of death on lips and brow,
And sank and sank . . . while still, as in a grave,
In the close dark beneath the crushing cart
He lay and listened to the far-off sea.
Wave after wave was knocking at his heart
And swishing, swishing, swishing ceaselessly
About the wain – cool waves that never reached
His cracking lips to slake his hell-hot thirst . . .
Shrill in his ears a startled barn-owl screeched . . .
He smelt the smell of oil-cake . . . when there burst
Through the big barn's wide-open door the sea –
The whole sea sweeping on him with a roar . . .
He clutched a falling rafter dizzily . . .
Then sank through drowning deeps to rise no more.

Down, ever down, a hundred years he sank
Through cold green death, ten thousand fathom deep.
His fiery lips deep draughts of cold sea drank
That filled his body with strange icy sleep
Until he felt no longer that numb ache,
The dead-weight lifted from his legs at last –
And yet he gazed with wondering eyes awake
Up the green glassy gloom through which he passed,
And saw far overhead the keels of ships
Grow small and smaller, dwindling out of sight,
And watched the bubbles rising from his lips,
And silver salmon swimming in green night,
And queer big golden bream with scarlet fins
And emerald eyes and fiery-flashing tails,
Enormous eels with purple-spotted skins,
And mammoth unknown fish with sapphire scales
That bore down on him with red jaws agape
Like yawning furnaces of blinding heat ;
And when it seemed to him as though escape
From those hell-mouths were hopeless, his bare feet
Touched bottom, and he lay down in his place
Among the dreamless legion of the drowned,
The calm of deeps unsounded on his face

And calm within his heart, while all around
Upon the midmost ocean's crystal floor
The naked bodies of dead seamen lay,
Dropped sheer and clean from hubbub brawl and roar
To peace too deep for any tide to sway.

. . . .

The little waves were lapping round the cart
Already when they rescued him from death.
Life cannot touch the quiet of his heart
To joy or sorrow as, with easy breath
And smiling lips, upon his back he lies
And never speaks or rises from his bed,
Gazing through those green glooms with happy eyes
While gold and sapphire fish swim overhead.

BEFORE THE WIND

Aboard her craft once more, she breathed the air
Of hard-won freedom : standing by to take
Her trick at the helm, she watched green-water break
Over the bow ; and, as she took the wheel,
Thrilled to its tug and wrench and the mate's 'Take care
She doesn't gybe !' and thrilled again to feel
The exultant sea-lift as the slicing keel
Cut clean the flaking foamheads – body and mind
Braced, mettled and strung tensely as the taut
Mainsheet, to keep the ship before the wind,
Enraptured to escape from brooding, caught
Into the conflict of the wind and wave
That shook her soul free from the thrall of thought,
The dire obsession of futility
That for so long had darkened all her life :
And now she felt at last that she was free,
Recovering in the elemental strife
Her own identity and the zeal to save

Her soul alive. Clear-eyed, with tossing hair
And lifted brow, she breathed the sharp salt air,
Nerved to an urgency that held her mind
Steady on even keel, and proud to find
Her seamanship sufficing still to keep
Through the blind smother and welter of the deep
The cutter running well before the wind.

THE FISHWIFE

The slush is ankle-deep in the street
Outside ; and the night is a flurry of sleet.
On slime-dank flags of the market she stands,
Serving with purple chilblained hands
Clammy and slithery soles, as she
Has stood the whole day patiently,
A squat broad bundle, fat and old,
With body and mind benumbed with cold.

And yet, when I caught the glint of her eye,
I saw a sprig of lass, half-shy,
Half-cheeky, who stood on the edge of the sea,
As the boats came in, and smiled to me –
A slip of a lass, with the curve of a sail,
As she leant her body against the gale,
And a head that tossed its hair like spray
In the light of the windy break of day.

And I know that bundle of clothes holds yet
The heart of a girl who cannot forget.

ON THE QUAY

Stifled all day by suffocating fluff
That filled the humming mill – at sunset free
She sauntered downward to the windy quay,
To clear her breathing of the choking stuff,
And rid her nostrils of the reek of jute,
Her senses, of the droning of the mill :
And she rejoiced to hear the eager hoot
Of the incoming whalers ; and to fill
Her lungs with briny savours ; and to see
The bearded salt-encrusted venturers
Whose hearts had dared the sheer immensity
Of the whales' playground ; and whose life, to hers –
Tied to a rattling loom through all her days
In a sick humid smothering atmosphere –
Seemed life, indeed, in shattering bright ways
Of wind-sheared shivering waters, tossing clear
To limitless horizons . . .

                                        And to-night,
Sparking, aware and eager eyed, she saw
The still blue eyes of a young whaler light
As he looked into hers ; and sudden awe
Filled her young heart, as though the very sea,
Darkling and dangerous, claimed her for its bride,
And salt tumultuous waters thunderously
Crashed drowning over her, tide after tide.

COASTER

Blindly we steal
Through the blind night with ship's lamps dully gleaming
And siren screaming,
And now a sudden whirling wheel
And a sharp signal tinkling
To warn the engineer
As in a twinkling
We shift our course and steer
On the port-tack or the starboard-tack, to clear
A bottom-ripping reef or the too near
Suddenly looming ghost
That bears down on us threateningly
With bows that barely sheer
Clear of catastrophe –
Blindly we steal
With cautious searching keel
Along the unseen coast
Through the obscurity
Of blind white night
Momently mantling with the eerie gleam
Of the far Longstone Light
Whose baffled beam
Can scarcely pierce the fog ; while everywhere
About us the incessant blare
Of sirens rends the shuddering numb air
With shriek and moan and howl
As unseen groping coasters prowl
So close we feel their wash about our hull.

And now an instant lull
When nothing stirs the brooding mystery
That merges sky and sea
Save the sharp eldritch yelling of a gull
Whole solitary railing
Sounds like the desolating scream
Of nightmare terror wailing
When the lost spirit, in uneasy sleep,

Still plunges desperately more deep
In suffocating labyrinths of fear :
Then, as the soul wakes and in smothering dread
Lies scarcely realising on the bed
That the familiar and dear
Daylight is glowing through the window-blind,
We seem to waken suddenly to find
The sea and sky swept clear
To the horizon and the summer night
Alive with glancing airs and scattering light
Beneath a heaven miraculous with stars ;
And as we waken from blind dream
Our dazed eyes dazzle to the gleam
Of the far Longstone's wheeling beam
That like a flourished scimitar's
Cold flashing cuts the crystalline
Blue lucency of June midnight :
And like souls newly won
Through the blind regions of oblivion
We stand beneath the dripping spars
And in divine
And quivering delight
Drink deep the quick air tanged with brine.

LUCK

What bring you, sailor, home from the sea –
Coffers of gold and of ivory ?

When first I went to sea as a lad
A new jack-knife was all I had :

And I've sailed for fifty years and three
To the coasts of gold and of ivory :

And now at the end of a lucky life
Well, still I've got my old jack-knife.

HOME

MOVING HOUSE

When the martins come next year
To their old nest in the gable,
They will never miss us, dear,
Never know that we're not here :
Strangers, rising from our bed,
Strangers, sitting at our table –
Yet they'll not guess we are fled.

Men, to birds, when all is said,
Are but men ; and they'll not mind
Who's the tenant, if they're able
'Neath the gable-peak to find
Their old nook. We'll leave behind
Little that will miss us, dear,
Save the old horse in the stable ;
And I doubt if he next year
Will recall that we lived here.

HOME

RETURN

Under the brown bird-haunted eaves of thatch
The hollyhocks in crimson glory burned
Against black timbers and old rosy brick,
And over the green door in clusters thick
Hung tangled passion-flowers when we returned
To our own threshold, and with hand on latch
We stood a moment in the sunset gleam
And looked upon our home as in a dream.

Rapt in a golden glow of still delight,
Together on the threshold in the sun
We stood, rejoicing that we two had won

To this deep golden peace ere day was done,
That over gloomy plain and storm-swept height
We two, O Love, had won to home ere night.

CANDLE-LIGHT

Where through the open window I could see
The supper-table in the golden light
Of tall white candles – brasses glinting bright
On the black gleaming board, and crockery
Coloured like gardens of old Araby –
In your blue gown against the walls of white
You stood adream, and in the starry night
I felt strange loneliness steal over me.

You stood with eyes upon the candle-flame
That kindled your thick hair to burnished gold
As in a golden spell that seemed to hold
My heart's love rapt from me for evermore . . .
And then you stirred, and, opening the door,
Into the starry night you breathed my name.

FIRELIGHT

Against the curtained casement wind and sleet
Rattle and thresh, while snug by our own fire
In dear companionship that naught may tire
We sit – you listening, sewing in your seat,
Half-dreaming in the glow of light and heat,
I reading some old tale of love's desire
That swept on gold wings to disaster dire,
Then sprang re-orient from black defeat.

I close the book, and louder yet the storm
Threshes without. Your busy hands are still,
And on your face and hair the light is warm
As we sit gazing on the coals' red gleam
In a gold glow of happiness, and dream
Diviner dreams the years shall yet fulfil.

MIDNIGHT

Between the midnight pillars of black elms
The old moon hangs, a thin cold amber flame
Over low ghostly mist : a lone snipe wheels
Through shadowy moonshine droning ; and there steals
Into my heart a fear without a name
Out of primeval night's resurgent realms,
Unearthly terror chilling me with dread
As I lie waking wide-eyed on the bed.

And then you turn towards me in your sleep,
Murmuring, and with a sigh of deep content
You nestle to my breast, and over me
Steals the warm peace of you ; and, all fear spent,
I hold you to me sleeping quietly
Till I too sink in slumber sound and deep.

1914-15

NOW TURN AND GO TO SLEEP AGAIN

Now turn and go to sleep again : there's nothing to be scaring you.
What is there to be fearing more in darkness than daylight ?
The wind that prowls around the house is just the wind that prowls around :
You never heeded it by day, and why should you by night ?

It's not the wind that's scaring you ? Ah, no use to be talking, then :
But I'll be sleeping sound enough, I warrant, till daylight.
I've kept my pecker up all day ; and faced the odds ; and I have earned
A long deep rest from watching, and a still unbroken night.

Now turn and go to sleep again : there's nothing to be scaring you.
What is there to be fearing more in darkness than daylight ?
The wind that wanders round the grave is just the wind that wanders round :
You never dreaded it by day, and why should you by night ?

127

WITHIN THE ROOFLESS STEADING...

Within the roofless steading
We lay that summer night,
Dry heather for our bedding,
And stars for candlelight.

We lay in the warm heather,
And watched the stars above,
Till we were drawn together
In the deep sleep of love.

Beneath the starry awning
We slumbered, breast to breast,
Until soft rain at dawning
Awakened us from rest :

And we arose ; and slipping
Our clothes off by the dyke,
Greeted the day by dipping
Our bodies in the syke.

THE WHITE COTTAGE

The cottage has a fresh coat of limewash,
And walls and roof, that, but the other day,
Were weathered grubby grey,
Flash white as marble in the summer moonshine.

Seth took a half-day off before his wedding,
To wash the old stones of his new home white
For Eleanor's delight,
And bridal-white they gleam in summer moonshine :

And on the first white night of life together
By their own hearthstone, warm the windows glow
In walls of glistering snow,
And mingle firelight gold with silver moonshine.

128

PLANTING BULBS

Work slack at his accustomed job, Old Nick
The coffin-maker tills
His little plot, and sets it thick
With bulbs of daffodils
And crocuses and squills.

He smiles, as in rich mould he sets each dry
And wizened bulb with care,
As though already to his eye
The flowers are blooming there,
And flourishing and fair :

For, looking past December's sleet and snow,
His heart already thrills
To see his cottage garden grow
Alive with daffodils
And crocuses and squills.

THE SEARCH

I've searched in every place that I can think of,
Ransacking the whole house, floor after floor,
Till, now I've looked so long, I've nigh forgotten
What I was looking for.

I've climbed up from the basement to the attic ;
And, as I pause for breath outside the door,
I'm wondering if I'll find, when it swings open,
Something worth looking for.

WATTLE-AND-DAUB

He slaps the daub against the wattle ;
And whistles gaily,
Happy because his little cottage
Is growing daily –
The little house of withes and loam
Is daily growing to a home.

He whistles gaily as a blackbird
A moment resting
To sing out, on a leafing willow,
The joy of nesting –
The joy that quivers in his breast
To be alive, and build a nest.

So, slapping daub against the wattle,
Ben's heart is singing,
Because each flourish of his trowel
Nearer is bringing
The happy day he'll bring her home
To their snug house of withes and loam.

GONE BUT NOT FORGOTTEN

THE LILAC TREE

Time had not left her soul unscarred :
Earning her bread
At twelve, and wed
At eighteen, she had had to struggle hard
To rear her thirteen children and to keep
Her ever-ailing husband, never free
An instant from anxiety
Or getting a full night's untroubled sleep –
Yet, as she scoured her little yard,
That morning when the lilac-tree
In crystal airs of Spring
Shook out its purple blooms, she turned to me
And said with eyes that sparkled happily
"I've always loved to work beside a living thing."

NO GRAVEN STONE

No graven stone
Marked her last bed ;
But at her head
A lilac-tree.
Where all alone
She'd made her bed
A lilac shed
Its fragrancy
Above her head.
No stone, she said
No stone for me :
When I alone
Lie quietly
Set my head
No lifeless stone :
But plant instead
A living tree.

GONE BUT NOT FORGOTTEN

"But not forgotten…" On the lichened stone,
Sunk half-awry in the neglected grave,
The words are barely legible, the words
That, newly cut, once looked so stout and brave –

That meant so much that desolate day to hearts
Bereft of her who'd given them life : and yet
The very life she'd given, it was, that surged
So strong in them, and helped them to forget.

Caught in the swirl of life that with new lives
Affianced theirs, that newer lives might be,
They brooded less and less upon the dead
And the memorials of mortality.

"But not forgotten . . ." while the race is run :
And lives that from her life sprung keep the track,
Although her name must perish, she yet lives
In hearts that never falter or turn back.

THE NAMELESS HEADSTONE

Above the time-obliterated mound
Still stands the headstone : but the graven name
Has all shaled off : and no man may recall
Who is the tenant of this little plot.

Yet when he died the world came to an end –
The world whose centre was his consciousness,
A world of hills and rivers, field and woods,
Sunlit and starry skies, a world of men,
Of loves and hates and dreams and ecstasies,
An individual world that only in
His heart existed – his heart that in its compass
Held a whole universe by God created
For him and him alone, by God who died
Within him as the light failed, and as all
The imagination of his heart was darkened . . .

132

Yet of the man and of the universe
That perished with his passing no memorial
Remains, save this blank shaling slab of stone.

THE FATHER

Disturbed at midnight on her lonely bed,
Within the circle of the nightlight's dim
Unwavering glow
She saw her husband stand, as though
Quite unexpectedly
He had returned on leave from oversea ;
And had it in her mind to speak to him –
Then shrank in dread ;
For, as she watched him lean
With eyes that glistened tenderly
Over the cot wherein was sleeping fast
Their newborn baby he had never seen,
His stooping head
No shadow on the lighted ceiling cast.

THE REFRAIN

I hear the clicking latch, the creaking door,
And hobnails grating on the sanded floor,
A dozen times a day – and yet he comes no more.

His hand has clicked that latch, and creaked that door,
His hobnails grated on the sanded floor,
Times out of mind – and yet he comes no more.

And now the latch aye clicks, and creaks the door,
And his sons' hobnail boots on the sanded floor
Grind out my heart's refrain – *He comes no more !*

CATCLEUCH SHIN

We met at dawn at Carter Bar
And climbed the Catcleuch Shin,
And talked of all that we had lost,
And all we hoped to win.

We talked and dreamed and talked and dreamed
Daylong among the bent,
Of all that life had done to us,
And all that it had meant.

Cloud-shadows swept o'er Kielder Head
And over Carter Fell ;
And when at last we rose to go
There seemed no more to tell.

But since upon our several ways
We parted silently,
Life, that had taken love from him,
Has given love to me.

Now while he's lying dead in France
With all he hoped to win,
My love and I from Carter Bar
Climb up the Catcleuch Shin.

ACKNOWLEDGEMENTS

Many thanks to the Wilfrid Gibson Literary Estate for permission to reproduce the poems and to Judy Greenway, Wilfrid Gibson's granddaughter, for her advice and assistance with the planning of this book; also by allowing the reproduction of some of her family photographs we learn more about the writer and his family.

To find out more about Judy Greenway and her work please see her web site – www.judygreenway.org.uk

Dr Roger Hogg has been extremely generous by sharing his research on Gibson; his knowledge has been invaluable. Dr Hogg's foreword introduces readers to the life and work of Wilfrid Gibson.

For further reading –
Hogg, Roger, 1990, *Wilfrid Wilson Gibson, People's Poet*: A critical and biographical study of W. W. Gibson 1878 - 1962, PhD thesis, University of Newcastle Upon Tyne.

Grateful thanks to Gaynor Scandle for all her hard work and patience with design and production; also many thanks to Gill Whatmough for proof reading.

Thank you to John Speight for permission to reproduce one of his original paper cuts on page 103. To see more of John's work go to his web site – www.johnspeight.co.uk

THE FRIENDS OF THE DYMOCK POETS

In the years leading up to the First World War, literary history was being made around the village of Dymock in Gloucestershire. Six poets stayed here, three of them lived here with their families.

Amidst orchards, woods and pastures, characterised by wild daffodils still to be found here, they laid the foundations for some of their finest poetry. They drew inspiration from this rural landscape and the local culture, but when the war came, their lives were changed forever.

They were :
>Rupert Brooke
>John Drinkwater
>Robert Frost
>Wilfrid Gibson
>Edward Thomas

Lascelles Abercrombie & Gibson lived in Ryton, where they published "New Numbers", a poetry magazine including their own verses with poems of Rupert Brooke and & John Drinkwater. Only four editions were produced in 1914 including the first publication of Rupert Brooke's famous sonnets.

American Robert Frost and family lived on the other side of Dymock, where Edward Thomas also stayed as he developed his own poetic voice. This brief period was ended by WWI.

www.dymockpoets.org.uk
Email : contact@dymockpoets.org.uk

GLOSSARY

bent-land – rough grassland or heathland
burn – small stream
cheapjack – seller of inferior goods, typically at a fair
corncrake – a bird; or a rattle sounding like a corncrake
cote – cottage or shelter
crag – steep or rugged cliff edge
crowberries – heather-like dwarf shrub with black berries
crowder – musician used to playing to crowds
daub – plaster, clay and straw mixture applied to laths or wattles to form a wall
dogcart – horse drawn two wheeled cart
fairing, faldalal, whigmaleerie – cheap fairground gifts
furze – gorse
ghyll – deep ravine, usually in woodland
greenjacks and jargonels – small sweet pears
greet – weep or cry
hags – soft area on a moor
happed – cover or wrap with warm clothes
herd – shepherd
hind – skilled farm worker
hiring – biannual fair where farmers and workers agree terms of employment
hoolet – owl
hopping – a fair
knar – knot or protuberance on a tree trunk or root
landrail – corncrake, a native bird inhabiting coarse grassland
lanthorn – early spelling of horn lantern
light-coats – fox hounds with pale coloured fur
ling – heather
linn – waterfall
mangel-wurzels – large type of beet used for animal feed
mould – loose earth and soil
outby – out-by, land away from farm, as opposed to in-by, close to the farm
pele – peel, small square defensive tower built in 16th century
penny-ice – small serving of ice cream served in a shallow glass
pitchy – like or as dark as pitch
plaid – a long piece of tartan wool cloth worn around shoulders
sallows – low growing or shrubby trees like willows
settle – a wooden bench with back and arms
small-pipes – Northumbrian pipes
stell – stone enclosure for animals
stife – smelly unpleasant atmosphere
stravaging – wander about aimlessly
syke – a small stream
tan-pits – tanning pits where leather is stained with oak bark
the Sele – public park in centre of Hexham
thrapple – throat
wain – horse wagon or cart
wattle – interlaced rods or stakes and branches to form a wall
whin – gorse
wiseacre – someone who considers himself knowledgeable; a know-all
withes and loam – building materials such as willow and clay, sand and vegetation
yeanling – young lamb or goat.

Northumbrian references:

Stagshaw Bank Fair – ancient cattle and sheep fair held a few miles north of Corbridge, Northumberland. This popular social event attracted many local folk with its sideshows, stalls and fairground.

The Whin Sill – a tabular layer of igneous rock dolerite stretching across northern England.

Cawfield Crag – crag on the Whin Sill, near Hadrian's Wall

Yeavering Bell – an ancient Iron Age hillfort

Thirlwall & Dunstanborough/Dunstanburgh – ruined castles

Fallowfield Fell & Catcleugh Shin – hills

Skirlnaked/Skirl Naked – remote cottage near Wooler

Carter Bar – a crossing over the border hills between Scotland and England.

SOURCES OF FEATURED POEMS

THE NETS OF LOVE 1905 (Elkin Mathews)
The Lambing   *The Haymakers*

THE WEB OF LIFE 1908 (Samurai Press)
In The Orchard   *The Mushroom-Gatherers*

FIRES 1912 (Elkin Mathews)

Flannan Isle	*The Dancing Seal*	*The Lilac Tree*
Red Fox	*Devil's Edge*	

THOROUGHFARES 1914 (Elkin Mathews)

Solway Ford	*The Ice*	*The Vixen*

BATTLE 1915 (Elkin Mathews)

Breakfast	*Hill-Born*	*The Quiet*
Hit	*Raining*	*The Father*
Comrades	*Worlds*	*Back*
Nightmare	*Desert Night*	

FRIENDS 1916 (Elkin Mathews)

The Ice-Cart	*Gold*	*The Orphans*
Rupert Brooke	*To The Memory of Rupert Brooke*	
Trees	*For G*	

LIVELIHOOD 1917 (Macmillan)

To Audrey	*The Old Piper*	*Skirlnaked*
The Old Nail-Shop	*In The Meadow*	*The Paisley Shawl*
The Plough	*Ralph Lilburn*	*Yeavering Bell*

WHIN 1918 (Macmillan)

Clattering Ford	*Before the Wind*	*Whistling Wind*
Whin	*Northumberland*	*Devilswater*
Catcleugh Shin	*The Crowder*	
The Happy Way	*Otterburn*	

138

HOME 1920 (Beaumont Press)

One-Day-Old	*Home*
To Audrey	*Michael*

NEIGHBOURS 1920 (Macmillan)

Ellen Chester	*Sam Hogarth*	*To Michael*
Betty Riddle	*Old Meg*	*Reveille*
Bessie Stokoe	*Witch's Linn*	*The Stair*

COLLECTED POEMS 1905-1925, 1926 (Macmillan)

Dunstanborough	*Lament*	*Thirlwall*
Fallowfield Fell	*Bacchanal*	*Mother and Maid*
Luck	*Beauty for Ashes*	*The Rider of the White Horse*
The White Whippet	*Hewer of Wood*	*A Garland for Jocelyn*
At the Pit-Head	*Northern Spring*	*Ned Nixon and his Maggie*
Stars	*The Wind-Bells*	*Blooms*
Audrey	*The White Cottage*	*Sally Black and Geordie Green*
The Lonely Tree	*"Oh, What Saw You?"*	
To Michael	*Mother and Maid*	

THE GOLDEN ROOM AND OTHER POEMS 1928 (Macmillan)

Wattle and Daub	*The Stell*	*To John Drinkwater*
Sarah	*The Refrain*	*Presage of Winter*
The Fishwife	*The Counterpane*	*To Edward Marsh*
The Homers	*The Chimney*	*Gray's Inn*
Song in Rain	*The Crowberries*	*Russell Hillard Loines*
Curlew	*The Bearers*	*The Golden Room*
The Old Wife	*Dear, Oh Dear!*	*The Barley Mow*
The Lonely Inn	*Wild Bees had Built . .*	*Moving House*
Venus di Milo	*The Mower*	*The Good News*
The Immortal	*The Wind and the Rain*	*Brown Waters*
The Release	*On Cawfield Crag*	*He is Tender with the Beasts*
The Wren	*By Carmarthen Bay*	*The Shepherd I*
Water from the Hills	*The Arrowhead*	*Within the Roofless Steading*
Under the Shawl	*John Pattison Gibson*	*Now Turn and go to Sleep*

HAZARDS 1930 (Macmillan)

Snow in May	*The Luck*	*Planting Bulbs*
Gone but not Forgotten	*The Windy Night*	*No Graven Stone*
Aftermath	*November Gold*	*The Luck*
November 11th	*On the Quay*	*Dandy Jack*
Her Epitaph	*The Look-Out*	*The Human Cannon-Ball*
January Nightfall	*The Cheerful Sweep*	*The Nameless Headstone*

ISLANDS 1932 (Macmillan) *Jocelyn*
FUEL 1935 (Macmillan) *The Ponies*
COMING AND GOING 1938 (Oxford University Press) *The Fatigue*
THE ALERT 1941 (Oxford University Press) *The Shepherd II, In Hexham Abbey*
THE OUTPOST 1944 (Oxford University Press) *The Happy Flight*
SOLWAY FORD and other Poems 1945 (Faber and Faber) *The Unseen Rider, The Three Poets*

Please note that some poems may have been printed in various poetry collection